This painting of the Right Reverend Thaddeus Amat, C.M., was presented to the Chancery Archives of the Archdiocese of Los Angeles by the bishop's great grandniece, Mrs. Carmelita Burton of Santa Barbara. It was painted by Faustine Adam y Tous at Barcelona in 1873.

California's Reluctant Prelate

THE LIFE AND TIMES OF
RIGHT REVEREND THADDEUS AMAT, C.M.
(1811 - 1878)

by

Rev. Francis J. Weber

"Pray for your bishop that the burden he was reluctant to accept, he may not be reluctant to bear."

DAWSON BOOK SHOP . . . 1964 . . . LOS ANGELES

96845

Nihil Obstat:
NEWMAN C. EBERHARDT, C.M.
Censor Deputatus
June 1, 1963

Imprimatur:
+TIMOTHY MANNING
Auxiliary Bishop of Los Angeles
Vicar General
June 6, 1963

CONTENTS

PAGE

Foreword ix
Preface xi

CHAPTER ONE
The Early Years... 1

CHAPTER TWO
Bishop of Monterey...................................... 29

CHAPTER THREE
The Franciscan Controversies 51

CHAPTER FOUR
The Pious Fund of the Californias....................... 73

CHAPTER FIVE
Diocesan Expansion 85

CHAPTER SIX
Religious and Educational Foundations................... 115

CHAPTER SEVEN
Catholic Collegiate Education in Southern California........ 137

CHAPTER EIGHT
Saint Vibiana and her Cathedral......................... 157

CHAPTER NINE
Amat at the First Vatican Council....................... 171

CHAPTER TEN
Bishop of Monterey-Los Angeles......................... 187

Bibliography 223
Index 231

v

ILLUSTRATIONS

PAGE

Right Reverend Thaddeus Amat, C.M. (painting) ....Frontispiece

Iglesia del Nuestra Senora del Pino, Barcelona 99

Eglise et Seminaire des Carmes, Paris 100

Saint Charles Seminary, Philadelphia 101

Private Oratory, old Urban College of Propaganda Fide 102

Document attesting to bestowal of the relics of Saint Vibiana .. 103

Formal opening of First Vatican Council, December 8, 1869 ... 104

Spanish translation of Amat's Tract on Matrimony 105

Iglesia de San Miguel del Puerto in Barcelona,
model for St. Vibiana's Cathedral in Los Angeles 106

Saint Vibiana's Cathedral in 1876 107

Interior view of Saint Vibiana's Cathedral in the 1880's 108

Relics of Saint Vibiana enshrined in ornate silver
reliquary, Saint Vibiana's Cathedral 109

Death notice of Right Reverend Thaddeus Amat, C.M. 110

Tomb of Bishop Amat in vault of Saint Vibiana's Cathedral... 111

Amat Crypt at Calvary Mausoleum 112

Title page of Amat's pastoral of December 28, 1855 113

FOREWORD

AMONG the historical writings pertaining to the Catholic Church in California during the nineteenth century, this biography of the Right Reverend Thaddeus Amat, C.M., merits a high place.

The author has spared no pains in making a thorough study of pertinent documents in Spain, France and Italy to say nothing of California and the United States. He presents here an instructive, interesting and inspiring portrayal of the life, times and works of an outstanding prelate and furnishes valuable references to such important matters as development of education, expansion of charitable and social agencies and the general evolution of ecclesiastical activities in California. In a word, he offers the reader a precious mine of information regarding the Catholic Church in nineteenth century California.

In addition to its serving as a biographical sketch, this volume treats of other inspiring figures on the California scene during the past century. The names of Joseph Sadoc Alemany O.P., Gonzales Rubio, O.F.M. and Francis Mora are among others whose deeds are written in letters of gold on the state's Catholic register.

Among his contemporaries, Thaddeus Amat is worthy of special attention by reason of his great sanctity, profound learning, consummate prudence and remarkable confidence in Divine Providence. An ardent zeal for the glory of God and the salvation of souls was his mission in life.

May this biography in its clear, forceful and elegant style enjoy a wide circulation! May it have an honored place in many libraries!

VERY REVEREND WILLIAM SLATTERY, C.M.

Superior General, Congregation of the Mission.

PREFACE

During much of the past century two cultural traditions, the Spanish-Mexican and the Anglo-American, were in conflict in Southern California. In most other areas of the Southwest, Anglos, Hispanos and Indians have happily managed to achieve mutual respect and accommodation, but in Southern California[1] the dichotomy has frequently been the cause of unfortunate conflicts. One recent historian has remarked that "according to official legend, the last vestiges of Spanish influences were obliterated when the conquering gringos overran the land."[2] As a matter of fact, this influence, although dormant for many years, was never completely extinguished, nor did the struggle for cultural accommodation cease with the American conquest.

Traditionally, the conflict between Anglo and Hispano has been confined to Southern California for Spanish-Mexican influence does not normally extend north of Tehachapi in Kern County. There are numerous Spanish place-names in the northern and central areas of the state, but

[1] *California del Sur,* or Southern California properly speaking is one of the smallest geographic regions in the United States. It includes part of Santa Barbara County (the portion of Tehachapi), all of Ventura, Los Angeles and Orange Counties and those portions of San Bernardino, Riverside and San Diego counties west of the San Bernardino Mountains. The area itself embraces approximately 11,729 square miles.

[2] Carey McWilliams, *Southern California Country* (New York, 1946), p. 49.

the preponderance of these names has been in the south where the Spanish-speaking population has always resided. The survival of Spanish influence in Southern California is in many ways attributable to the discovery of gold which, for all practical purposes, divided California into two states.[3] In the three decades after 1849 thousands of Americans invaded the northern parts of the state but Southern California remained virtually unchanged, a condition illustrated by the continued use of the Spanish language throughout the 1860's and 1870's. As late as 1869, Los Angeles was hardly more than a small Mexican town in which Spanish was spoken almost exclusively. As a result of this time-lag in social change, Spanish-Mexican influences struck deeper roots in the south than elsewhere in California. In fact, it was not until the great influx of population in the 1880's that conditions finally began to change.

The present study endeavors to depict, in biographical form, the development of ecclesiastical jurisdiction in Southern California during the quarter-century episcopate (1854-1878) of the Right Reverend Thaddeus Amat, C.M., who was himself a Spaniard by birth and a man eminently qualified to wear the mitre in the late years of Southern California's Spanish-Mexican predominance. It has been said that the influence of the Catholic Church was relatively greater in California than anywhere else in the United States during the period.[4] Allowing for exaggeration in that statement, we would still be warranted in as-

[3]As far back as the mission era, the friars suggested that the state should be divided for administrative purposes at the Tehachapi line. A proposal was advanced at the first session of the Mexican legislature in 1822 to divide the area. In 1851, a convention for the same purpose met in Los Angeles and in 1859 the people of Southern California, by a two-thirds vote, approved a measure for division which was forwarded to Congress. Proposals to this effect have continued to be made at frequent intervals in later years.

[4]Nellie Van de Grift Sanchez, *California: The Hispanic Period* (Chicago, 1926), p. 550.

suming that the man most responsible for that Catholic influence was the local bishop.

In this particular study, the unfortunate lack of primary material made it necessary to travel extensively through the United States and Europe in order to substantiate our findings. And in this regard we are extremely grateful to His Eminence, James Francis Cardinal McIntyre, for allowing this research to continue, both by his moral encouragement and financial assistance. His Excellency the Most Reverend Timothy Manning, Vicar General of the Archdiocese of Los Angeles, was the *causa motivans* of this study as well as other related historical pursuits and to him is due a special debt of gratitude.

A number of people gave most generously of their time and talents in helping this biographical sketch through its more perilous days. We would single out for mention the Right Reverends John Tracy Ellis and Benjamin G. Hawkes, the Reverends Bartholomew F. Fair, Maynard J. Geiger, O.F.M., Bernard J. McCoy, C.M., John B. McGloin, S. J., Robert Trisco and John Zimmerman, C.M., all of whom graciously assisted by furnishing the writer with source material from the archival deposits of which they are custodians or in other ways furthered the preparation of this work. It should be noted, however, that none of the above saw the book in its final form and since many of their observations were not incorporated, their names must be disentangled from any responsibility for what appears in the treatise.

—REV. FRANCIS J. WEBER.

CHAPTER ONE

THE EARLY YEARS

Barcelona, once the proud capital of the Kingdom of Catalonia, and known even today among Spaniards as the "Queen of the Mediterranean" was founded in 225 B.C. and within twenty years was elevated to the status of a colony in the Roman Empire. The ancient city was built atop the Taber Hill where stands today the magnificent Santa Eulalia Cathedral, a church thought to be one of the noblest creations of Spanish Gothic. Her days of greatest splendor came when Barcelona was constituted head of the Catalan-Argonese monarchy, a period during which the "Queen City" assimilated the cultures of the East and West with such proficiency as to achieve a flourishing municipal life and a wide and vigorous political, military and commercial expansion.

This great center of Spanish culture is of special interest to students of California Catholicism for Catalonia not only provided many of the early Franciscan missionaries but it also gave three of its native sons to the California hierarchy,[5] all cultivated churchmen who shared their noble Catalan heritage with the Church in the Western United States.

[5]*Viz.*, Joseph Sadoc Alemany, O.P., Thaddeus Amat, C.M. and Francis Mora.

Barcelona has never abounded in outstanding individuals or dominating classes but her people have always possessed an intelligent, realistic, disciplined, stubborn and hard working attitude toward the problems of daily life. A typically practical, optimistic and progressive family in Barcelona at the turn of the nineteenth century was that of Pedro Amat and Maria Brusi.

Tracing their ancestry back to the eighth century,[6] the Amats of Barcelona had every reason to boast of their illustrious predecessors. There was an Amat in the Army of Charles Martel when he marched into Catalonia in the 740's. The family established itself in a large manor house in the Queen City and was to occupy a prominent place in society from that time on. Descendants soon spread into the neighboring villages of Palou, Castellvell and Labastida and formed three distinct branches. At the beginning of the fourth century, the annals list three Amats as commissioners of Barcelona, Francisco, Ramon and Pedro. The latter was a private chamberlain to King Martin I of Aragon. A great patron of the Church, it was Pedro Amat who donated the land in Barcelona where the stately Santa Maria de los Reyes (del Pino) was soon to take form.[7]

Five generations later, José Amat y Desbach, inheriting his family's close ties with the royalty, became chamberlain to King Phillip IV (1621-1665). Not an overly capable ruler, Phillip delegated broad authorities to his subordinates and José Amat soon assumed a position of vast influence within the realm. His son, Juan Amat y Despalau,

[6]Alberto Garcia Carraffa, *Diccionario Heraldico y Genealogico* (Madrid, 1921), pp. 49-55.

[7]Pedro Amat y Torre married Isabel Junyet. There were two sons, Romeu and Jaime. Thaddeus Amat was descended from Romeu. Luigi Cardinal Amat (1796-1878) traced his lineage to Jaime. That branch of the family subsequently was known as the Amats di San Filipo e Sorso of Aragon. Cf. *Dictionnaire d'Histoire et de Geographie Ecclesiastique*, II, 981 for a biographical sketch of the cardinal.

became a commissioner for Barcelona and held that pivotal office for three terms. With the elevation of his son to the same post, the office became hereditary. In the years after 1702, the senior male offispring of the Amat family inherited the title of Marquis di Castellvell,[8] a development which further added to their influence in public affairs.

It was then into a noble and tradition-filled family that Thaddeus Amat y Brusi came in the early years of the nineteenth century. No longer closely attached to the fortunes of the monarchy, the Amats nevertheless enjoyed a fine reputation in their community. Tadeo's father, Pedro, was a manufacturer of munitions[9] and was later to become a general in the Spanish guard. His mother, Maria Brusi, although born in Naples, had spent most of her life in Barcelona and was distantly akin to the famous family of that great name who founded the *Diario de Barcelona*, leading publication in all of Spain.

The regency of Joseph Bonaparte was nearing its end when Thaddeus Amat was born in the city which he would later refer to, in the words of Cervantes, as "the flower of the beautiful cities of the world,"[10] Barcelona. On the very day of his birth, Hagmanay, or Aguinaldo as it was known in Spain, December 31, 1811,[11] the infant was taken in the *camadrana* or minor procession to be baptized in the paro-

---

[8]On Bishop Amat's episcopal shield, the coat-of-arms of the Amats Castellvell form one side of the field.

[9]On Amat's baptismal entry, his father is identified as "armero." In 1962 a painting of General Amat de Capdevila was presented to the Archdiocese of Los Angeles by Mrs. Carmelita Burton of Santa Barbara, a great grandniece of Bishop Amat.

[10]Miguel de Cervantes, "Las Das Doncellas," *Obras Completas* (Madrid, 1949), p. 955.

[11]The certificate notes the date as *"treima y un de Desembre de mil vint cents y once"* (1811).

chial Church of Nuestra Señora del Pino.[12] The entry in the registers of the Church, as recorded by the parish priest in Catalan, notes that the youngster's name was bestowed in honor of the Apostle, Jude Thaddeus, who was and is greatly venerated in the 15th century basilica. If the normal customs of the time were observed, the godmother took the child, after the Baptismal ceremony,[13] to the Capilla de Santo Cristo in the nearby cathedral and dedicated him to the Lord beneath the crucified "Christ of Lepanto" which Don Juan of Austria is said to have carried on the prow of his flagship during the Battle of Lepanto.

RELIGIOUS LIFE

There is little information extant on the earliest years of Thaddeus Amat for the Spaniards of that era were not given to keeping diaries or journals as they were in a later day. Formal education was a luxury not enjoyed by the average Spanish boy and it remains a credit to his industrious father that Tadeo was able to acquire a fine elementary and secondary education. And in the process, he became proficient not only in his native Spanish and Catalan, but in French and Italian as well, to say nothing of his later mastery of Latin, Greek, Hebrew and English, all of which he spoke and wrote with great facility.

Early in his life, Tadeo seems to have become conscious of the tremendous need of the Church for zealous and dedicated priests. He was especially attracted to the

[12]The identity of this church was discovered in Benito Paradela, C.M., *Notas Biograficas de los que han pertenecido a la Congregacion de la Mision en España.* (Madrid, 1935), p. 157. *"En la partida de Bautismo que en 1924 vimos en la parroquia del Pino, de Barcelona, consta fue bautizado alli en 31 de diciembre de 1819."* This entry was checked personally by the author on October 23, 1962.

[13]People of those times formed a *camadrana* or minor procession to the Church. The term refers to *comare* (mid-wife) who customarily carried the infant.

spirit of Saint Vincent de Paul, whose motto, "God has sent me to preach to the poor,"[14] appealed to him as the greatest of human challenges. Thaddeus was also impressed by other features of the Vincentians, including their canonical status which allowed members to remain secular priests bound together in community by private vows. Saint Vincent had directed his followers to give themselves entirely to the various apostolic works to which zeal for God's glory might call them among either the clergy or the laity. This he had divided into two broad categories; the instruction of the poor and the direction of seminaries.

When he made known his desire to enter the community, Tadeo's parents readily acquiesced and in 1826 saw their son enrolled in the Apostolic College attached to the Casa Central in Madrid,[15] preparatory seminary for the Province of Lombardy. He remained there until the latter part of December, 1831.[16] Amat was received as a postulant in the Congregation of the Mission on January 4, 1832.[17]

Amat's novitiate consisted of two years of seclusion and discipline during which he made every effort to assimilate the spirit of Vincent de Paul. There were daily conferences by the Master of Novices, classes on the principles of Ascetical Theology, history of the community, obligations of religious life as well as exercises of meditation, spiritual

[14]The words *"Evangelizare pauperibus misit me"* appear on the official seal of the Congregation of the Mission.

[15]Archives of Juventude de la Medella Milagrosa (hereafter referred to as AJMM). Jose Herrera, C.M. to the author, Madrid, September 15, 1962. Father Herrera provided the author with fourteen pages of transcripts from the Madrid files but did not further specify the sources.

[16]Archives of Maison Mere (hereafter referred to as AMM), "Catalogue Sacerdotum et Clericorum Congregationis Missionis Americanae Provinciae, 1816." Entry No. 51, p. 32.

[17]AMM, "Dictionnaire Du Personnell Congregation de la Mission," Deuxieme Series, 1801-1900 (A-B), Book 446. Entry under AMAT, Taddee (458).

reading and exegesis of Sacred Scripture. Several hours each day were spent in physical labor in and around the house. All told, it was a fitting and worthy preparation through which only the most sincere candidates could pass. Finally, on January 16, 1834,[18] young Amat was ready to take the four vows which made him a member of the Congregation of the Mission. During Mass celebrated in Barcelona's Iglesia de Nuestra Señora de la Merced,[19] he made permanent his consecration in these words:

> Ego, THADDEUS AMAT, indignus clericus Congregationis Missionis coram beatissima virgine et curia coelesti universa voveo Deo, toto vitae tempore, paupertatem, castitatem et superiori nostro ejusque successoribus obedientiam, juxta Instituti nostri regulas seu Constitutiones, voveo praeterea me pauperum resticanorum saluti ad toto vitae tempore in dicta congregatione ejusdem Dei omnipotentis gratia adjuvante quem ob hoc suppliciter invoco.[20]

At the conclusion of the ceremony, Amat was a full-fledged Vincentian, with all the rights, duties and privileges accruing to followers of the great Apostle of Charity.

Thaddeus had been an outstanding student and his superiors recommended him for a teaching position where his erudition and pedagogical ability could be fully utilized. And while the young Vincentian was aware of his God-given talents in this particular field, his reading had stirred within him a strong desire for the active ministry where he could personally assist in the spiritual conquest for souls. After an extended retreat, Amat and his fellows knelt before the local bishop on May 23, 1834, to receive tonsure

[18]Benito Paradela, C.M., *op. cit.*, p. 158.

[19]Jose Herrera, C.M., *Historia de la Congregacion de la Mision* (Madrid, 1949), p. 235.

[20]*Formulary of Prayers* (Saint Louis, 1945), p. 37.

and the four minor orders.[21] It was a happy day for the young seminarian who repeated his dedication to the service of the Church in the age-old words:

Dominus pars, haereditatis meae, et calicis mei. Tu es, qui restitues haereditatem meam mihi.[22]

Within the year, he again marched into chapel, this time vested in alb and cincture, carrying a tunic where, after the chanting of the litany of the saints, he was ordained subdeacon, the first of the three great steps to the priesthood.

Meanwhile, the political atmosphere in Barcelona was worsening. With the defeat of the Carlists, the government of Queen Isabella II avenged itself of the Church for its support of Don Carlos by ordering the suppression of many religious houses throughout the realm. This, coupled to the earlier French occupation of the country, left a violent anti-clerical feeling among many people, especially the Liberals and Freemasons. Extreme measures against the Church were a common occurrence and ecclesiastical properties were being seized by the government in an obvious intent to nationalize the Spanish Church by degrees.

There were about fifty priests, students and brothers then living in the house on Calle Provenza where Amat was studying.[23] On the night of July 24, 1834, a mob stormed the house, killing one brother and wounding several others. The entire community was taken to the Castle of Montjuich[24] where they shared the unhappy lot of many other religious already in the prison. For fifteen days Amat and

[21]The practice of receiving tonsure and minor orders on the same day was declared illicit in 1918 when the new Code of Canon Law was promulgated.

[22]*Pontificale Romanum Summorum Pontificium* (Rome, 1873), p. 16.

[23]AJMM, Jose Herrera, C.M. to author, Madrid, September 15, 1962.

[24]The house in Barcelona was only reopened in 1867 when the property was restored to the Church. It is now the Provincial House of the Padres Paules for Barcelona.

his confreres suffered from hunger, exposure and insults. When word finally arrived that the inmates would be expelled from the country, Amat was among those chosen to go to Paris where the Vincentian Superior General, the Very Reverend Dominic Salhorgne had thrown open the doors of Maison-Mere.

Setting out from Barcelona in early August, Thaddeus and a small group of his fellow students journeyed through Perpignan, Carcassonne, Montelieu and Toulouse arriving at 95 rue de Sevres on November 15, after a long and exhausting journey.[25] The Spanish contingent was warmly welcomed at Paris where their modesty, silence and spirit of dedication contributed greatly to the community. So impressed were the French Lazarists with their Spanish counterparts, the Padres Paules, that a circular was later sent to all the provinces with these observations:

> We have received the Spaniards with the love that is inspired in us by their misfortune and the edifying resignation with which they bear it. There are twenty-one in our house in Paris and a similar number spread out among the houses in the south of France. We consider it a duty and a good fortune to soften as much as we can the bitterness of their pains and to console them in their unhappy exile. Our hospitality is amply compensated by the examples which they give us of all the virtues of our vocation. I do not doubt that their presence will serve to reawaken in us the spirit of Saint Vincent and bind more tightly the bonds of love that must unite all the members of the Congregation.[26]

Another observer had this comment about the Spanish exiles:

[25]AMM, "Catalogue General, Congregation de la Mission," Tome II, 1801-1900, 27.

[26]AJMM, Typed transcript of pastoral letter from Superior General. No date.

The Italian missioners preserve the cassock of Saint Vincent; the French have his body; but the Spaniards have his spirit.[27]

Amat was soon immersed in his work in the new Paris surroundings of the former Hotel des Lorges.[28] He seems to have been well liked by his superiors and was frequently called upon to assist those of his fellow-Spaniards not so familiar with the French language. He gave himself completely to his studies—almost to the point of fatigue, always motivated by a genuine intellectual curiosity. The intensity of his study would have ruined a less vigorous constitution. One of the rewards he soon discovered in his theological work was the realization that the most effectual manner of teaching the virtues and moral doctrine is to display them in one's own person. In scholastic training, Amat was to bring to the United States an academic background that few ecclesiastics in the young republic of that period could match. And, aside from the cultural advantages of his years in France, he was removed from the turbulence then ravaging his native land.

ORDINATION TO THE PRIESTHOOD

Thaddeus Amat was raised to the diaconate on May 30, 1837.[29] Through a special indult granted by the Holy See to the Congregation of the Mission, students attached to the central house in Paris were allowed the privilege of ordination midway through the final year of theology. Thus, on December 23, 1837,[30] Amat and his fellow deacons knelt

---

[27]*Ibid.*

[28]95 rue de Sevres has been the location of the Vincentian Motherhouse since 1817.

[29]AMM, "Catalogue. . . .," Entry No. 51, p. 32.

[30]For the interesting story behind the determining of this date, cf. Francis J. Weber, "Thaddeus Amat, Fact versus Fiction," *Records of The American Catholic Historical Society* LXXIV (September 1963).

before Hyacinthe Louis de Quelen, Archbishop of Paris, and listened to the Superior General solemnly respond to the interrogation concerning the worthiness of the candidates:

So far as human frailty allows one to know, I do know, that they are worthy to undertake the burdens of this office.

When he rose from the sanctuary floor,[31] Amat's mind may well have mirrored the thoughts of a contemporary, who was heard to say on a similar occasion, "one kneels in the consciousness of his own nothingness and arises a priest forever."[32]

Father Amat had finished his studies by early summer and then spent some weeks administering the sacraments in and around Paris. He was popular with the people wherever he went for he was no less adept at preaching than he was in the classroom. He had that rare ability of expressing the most difficult ideas in a language understandable to the simplest of his hearers.

MISSIONARY YEARS

On July 19, 1838, Feast of Saint Vincent de Paul, the young priest received his appointment to the recently established American Province.[33] He went at once to La Havre and after waiting there three weeks for favorable winds and high tides, Amat and his eight confreres set out on August 9 for New Orleans.[34] During the long voyage he gave himself to improving his English which, until now, he had never had occasion to speak. Lack of water, always

[31]The ordination took place in the present-day Chapel of Paris' Catholic University, Eglise Saint-Joseph des Carmes, December 23, 1837.

[32]A remark attributed to Saint John Vianney, the Cure of Ars.

[33]The American Province had been founded as a separate jurisdiction on September 2, 1835.

[34]Charles C. Conroy, The Centennial (Los Angeles, 1940), p. 22.

a rare commodity in the days when unpredictable winds could keep a ship at sea for weeks in excess of its supply of rations, was only one of the privations of the long and tiresome journey. The two month voyage was prolonged endlessly by exceedingly calm waters and delayed their arrival until,

> On October 20 a squall-slowed brig, plying between Havre and New Orleans, landed a band of nine volunteers from Saint-Lazare, most of them Spaniards.[35]

Almost immediately after his disembarking at New Orleans on October 20, Father Amat was assigned to the faculty of Assumption Seminary[36] located about eighty river miles down Bayou Lafourche near Donaldsonville. It was an agreeable assignment in many ways, for the building, a two-story brick edifice, had only recently been completed and offered conveniences not commonly expected in that area of the American Missions. Amat did not confine his activities solely to seminary routine but was frequently called upon by his superior, Father Bonaventure Armengol, to perform parochial duties at Assumption Church, fifteen miles away at Donaldsonville. He also gave considerable time to traversing a wide stretch of territory into the backwoods almost to the Atchafalaya River, visiting distant settlements and farms, instructing, assisting at marriages and burying the dead. The Vincentian annals contain an interesting letter written by Amat to the Superior General, Father John B. Nozo,[37] giving a remarkably

[35]Benito Paradela, C.M., *Resumen Historico de la Congregacion de la Mision en España desde 1704 a 1868* (Madrid, 1923), p. 307.

[36]Placed under the patronage of Saint Vincent de Paul, the seminary was more commonly referred to as "Assumption" the name of the parish within its immediate area. It was destroyed by fire in 1855 and rebuilt at a later date in New Orleans.

[37]*Annals de la Congregation de la Mission* (Paris, 1839), V, 83-87. Letter dated January 15, 1839.

detailed description of the spiritual status of Assumption parish, its population, growth and problems. On one of his mission journeys, the young Vincentian dedicated a small chapel and left this memento of his activity:

> I, Father Thaddeus Amat, authorized by Bishop Antoine Blanc, blessed, according to the rites of the Catholic Church, a small chapel built on the land of Mr. Vincent Leivicque by him in honor of Saint Vincent Ferrer for the benefit of all the Catholic surrounding.[38]

On March 5, 1841, Father Amat was sent to the American Province's motherhouse on the fringe of the Barrens Settlement in Perry County, Missouri to pursue his study of English.[39] The following month he went to Saint Vincent's College at Cape Girardeau as Director of Novices, a position of great importance in any community. During that year he imparted to his charges the principles of a deep spirituality built on a firm theological foundation.[40] 1842 found Amat again at Saint Mary-of-the-Barrens,[41] this time as rector, teaching and assisting in the contiguous Church of Saint Mary of the Assumption. This double duty was pleasant for Amat and he was successful in both endeavors. When the diocesan section of the seminary was moved to Saint Louis in October of 1842,[42] Father Amat was named administrator of the new foundation[43] and, at the

[38]Roger Baudier, *The Catholic Church in Louisiana* (New Orleans, 1939), p. 383.

[39]AJMM, Anonymous manuscript. Dated "Philadelphia, 1903."

[40]E. Pruente, "The Beginnings of Catholicity in Cape Girardeau," *Saint Louis Catholic Historical Review*, III (January-April, 1921), 73.

[41]AMM, "Registre des Conseils," I, 137. The appointment is dated November 4, 1841 but probably didn't reach Amat until the following January.

[42]*Ibid.*, I, 232. The *Catholic Almanac* for 1843 reads, "The Seminary heretofore connected with Saint Mary's College, Perry County, is now placed at Saint Louis."

[43]The appointment was dated November 4, 1842. John Timon, the provincial, was the *de facto* rector. Bishop Peter Richard Kenrick had great confidence in the future Bishop of Buffalo but apparently had little regard for Amat whom he had removed from office in 1844.

same time, pastor of the recently inaugurated parish of the Holy Trinity then housed in temporary quarters.[44] The seminary[45] was located nearby in the Antoine Souhard mansion on Bishop's Row.[46] Except for a brief span at Donaldsonville, Amat administered both the parish and seminary until 1844 when he was succeeded by Father Blasius Raho, C.M.,[47] who supervised the erection of a new church dedicated to Saint Vincent. On July 8, 1844,[48] Father John Timon[49] transferred Amat to Cape Girardeau as president of the seminary and superior of the community. "Father Amat filled the office of President for a year or more when he was transferred to the Barrens and made superior of that Institution."[50] Entries in the registers of Assumption Church in Perryville indicate the young priest's zeal for as superior of Saint Mary's Seminary[51] he was again re-

[44]Originally slated for Ninth and Marion streets where the cornerstone was placed in 1838, a new site was chosen in 1844 further north on Ninth street and the title of the parish changed to Saint Vincent. The *Catholic Almanac* mentions that Amat was also chaplain of Sacred Heart Convent.

[45]This seminary was the predecessor of present-day Kenrick Seminary at Webster Groves, Missouri.

[46]Cf. John Rothensteiner, *History of the Archdiocese of Saint Louis* (Saint Louis, 1928), I, 837 for a description o⁵ Amat. Among other things he states that Amat "was a rigid disciplinarian and consequently not very popular with the students. But he was a just man, a sound scholar and an excellent professor."

[47]Raho was later to become Vicar General of the Diocese of Monterey-Los Angeles.

[48]AMM, "Registre . . . ," I, 324.

[49]Timon was Amat's *mentor*. The two continued their friendship in later years but unfortunately most of Timon's papers were destroyed by a fire in Buffalo's old cathedral rectory according to the Reverend Ralph Bayard, C.M., author of Timon's biography.

[50]John Rothensteiner, *op. cit.*, II, 85. (From a series of articles in "Church of Progress" published at Saint Louis in 1894.) Amat's appointment was dated July 14, 1845. Cf. "Registre . . . ," I, 368.

[51]Saint Mary-of-the-Barrens Seminary was founded in 1818 and incorporated by the Missouri General Assembly in 1822. It 1830 it received the charter to grant educational degrees, the first institution of higher learning west of the Mississippi River and the first incorporated by state law.

sponsible for its attached church, a duty he carefully discharged.

It was in 1844 that the Superior General selected Father Bonaventure Armengol to head a new province of Spanish Vincentians in Mexico's capital city. The need for priests was great and various establishments offered to Armengol had to be turned down for no other reason than lack of personnel. The Bishop of Galveston, John Odin, himself a Vincentian, remarked in his journal that,

They are having a hard time finding Spanish confreres to send (to Mexico City). Mr. Etienne asked me whether I thought you could spare Mr. Amat; he felt afraid to mention anything about him to you knowing that you had not already subjects in sufficient number. I told him that though Mr. Amat was a very useful and well deserving member of the Congregation, you would at once let him go if the interests of the Congregation required it.[52]

Father Timon declined, however, to spare Amat whom he considered "one of the most valuable priests . . . lured to America."[53] In his place, the provincial sent four other priests and a lay brother.

Several years earlier, in 1832, Francis Patrick Kenrick, Coadjutor Bishop of Philadelphia, had established a small seminary which he housed next to the episcopal residence until larger quarters could be provided. It had been granted a charter by the Legislature of Pennsylvania in 1838, and the next year it was moved to its new headquarters at 18th and Race Streets. Control of the institution was entrusted to the Vincentians in July of 1841 by Bishop Kenrick who was well acquainted with the Vincentian Fathers and their establishment of Saint Mary's in Missouri which, at one time, had served the entire Louisiana area. In the

52Ralph Bayard, C.M., *Lone Star Vanguard* (Saint Louis, 1945), p. 351.
53*Ibid.*

early fall of 1847, the Very Reverend Mariano Maller, C.M., Rector of Saint Charles Seminary in Philadelphia, was named visitor, succeeding the Right Reverend John Timon, newly designated Bishop of Buffalo. The superiorship of Saint Charles was then given to Father Thaddeus Amat. And although his appointment was dated October 4, 1847,[54] he could not conclude his other duties and get to his new position until early the next year. The number of seminarians then was twenty-five and the total amount of subscriptions for the institution was $4,043.26.[55] In his first annual report, Amat expressed his personal feelings on the heavy burdens of his latest appointment when he wrote:

> It has fallen to my lot, with the approbation of the Bishop of the diocese, to fill the place of one whose devotedness to the best interests of the seminary, is appreciated by all who knew him; in whose footsteps it shall be my humble ambition to walk, relying next to God, on the continued cooperation of those who charity and zeal in the cause of religion, we are indebted for the present promising condition of the Institution.[56]

Father Amat's appointment to Philadelphia was received with considerable enthusiasm by both clergy and laity. According to the historian of the seminary

> His teaching and administrative ability, coupled with his special qualities as a spritual guide were widely acclaimed, and by the time he came to Philadelphia, he was well equipped in experience for the office awaiting him.[57]

[54]AMM, "Dictionnaire . . .," Book 446.

[55]Marc F. Vallete, "Brief Sketch of Saint Charles Borremeo Seminary," *United States Catholic Historical Magazine,* I, 24.

[56]Thaddeus Amat, C.M., *Annual Report of the Superior of the Theological Seminary of Saint Charles Borromeo of Philadelphia* (for the year ending November 4, 1848), p. 3.

[57]George O'Donnell, *Saint Charles Seminary* (Philadelphia, 1953), I, 30.

Among the first projects initiated by the new rector was a program to enlarge the seminary. He was distressed by the lack of accommodations, since as he said, "several other candidates for the holy ministry might have been received, if the adequate means for their support had been at our disposal."[58] Amat addressed his appeal directly to the laity of the diocese:

> We cannot too highly praise the grace of God vouchsafed to those who really love their religion and are willing to sacrifice some portion of their temporal goods for the salvation of their brethren.
>
> For as long as the Church has no other treasury than the charity of her faithful, manifestly great must be the influence either for good or evil, which her children's love towards her will exercise on her progress.[59]

By 1849, Amat had drawn plans for a new building to be erected facing Race Street and he repeatedly urged the necessity of such expansion to safeguard the health of the students and provide for an ever increasing enrollment. Nevertheless, he observed

> . . . The works of God generally proceed by very slow degrees, and often almost against hope do they toil and persevere who aspire to be the beneficiaries of their fellowmen, in building up Institutions which will continue to bless them, long after the patient hope, the self-denying labors of their founders have been forgotten.[60]

The appeal was heeded by Philadelphia's faithful and in 1850 construction was begun on a new seminary building which was a great joy to its rector and his small faculty. The new addition was spoken of by its rector in these glowing terms:

[58]Thaddeus Amat, C.M., *op. cit.*, p. 3.
[59]*Ibid.*, p. 4.
[60]*Ibid.*, (for the year ending November 4, 1849), p. 5.

The Theological Seminary of Saint Charles Borromeo has been much enlarged, both as regards the number of Ecclesiastical students, and the buildings appropriated to their use. It is now one of the most spacious and commodious seminaries in the United States, furnished with a valuable Theological Library, and with ample accommodations for as large a number of students as the multiplying wants of the Diocese will require.[61]

During his four-year rectorship in Philadelphia, Amat witnessed the expansion of Saint Charles Seminary, not only in physical size, but more important in its spiritual influence. Priests from the seminary were sent to all the corners of the nation and many of their names are now written in capital letters in local necrologies.

Amat became a close personal friend of Bishop Francis Patrick Kenrick, more so than with his brother, Peter Richard, under whom he had worked in Saint Louis. Amat accompanied Kenrick in 1849 to the Seventh Provincial Council of Baltimore as his personal theologian,[62] and it was a very real personal loss for Amat when Kenrick was promoted to the Premier See of Baltimore in September of 1851.

Kenrick's successor in Philadelphia was John N. Neumann, C.Ss.R., who received his appointment early the next year. Father Amat and a group of priests from the city went to Baltimore for the consecration of their new Ordinary on March 28, 1852. The ceremony took place in the historic cathedral and Amat, as rector of the seminary, took an active part in the functions.[63] At the conclusion of the ceremonies, it was Amat's privilege to escort the new bishop back to Philadelphia where the townspeople had

[61]Ibid., (for the year ending November 4, 1851), p. 3.

[62]Peter K. Guilday, A History of the Councils of Baltimore (New York, 1932), p. 156.

[63]Cf. North American and United States Gazette, March 30, 1852 for a description of the ceremony.

arranged an enthusiastic welcome for their new shepherd.[64]

Amat's name had been considered for the provincialate in April of 1846[65] when it was learned that the Holy See was about to erect a diocese at Buffalo and name John Timon its first bishop. No definitive action, however, was taken at that time and the appointment eventually went to the Reverend Mariano Maller whom Amat then succeeded in Philadelphia. It has also recently been discovered that the General Council at Paris named Thaddeus Amat Provincial and Director of the Daughters of Charity in the Madrid Province in 1848 to succeed Buenaventura Codina who had been elected Bishop of the Canaries.[66] But again there is no evidence that Amat ever was informed of this action.

It would have taken a far less perceptive man than John Neumann to realize that his seminary rector would eventually be "promoted out" of Philadelphia. Neumann had learned to rely heavily on Amat and when the First Plenary Council of Baltimore convened in May of 1852, he followed his predecessor's example in asking Amat to accompany him as theologian.[67] Here it would be that Amat was given to the nation, not just to a single diocese for it was at this council that the bishops proposed his name as one of the three possible successors to the Bishop of Monterey, Joseph Sadoc Alemany. This action, taken in private session greatly disconcerted the young Vincentian who had come to know from first-hand experience the anxieties and care of the episcopate.

[64]Michael J. Curley, C.Ss.R., *Venerable John Neumann (Fourth Bishop of Philadelphia)*, (Washington, 1952), p. 182.

[65]AMM, "Registre . . .," I, 395.

[66]*Ibid.*, I, 434.

[67]John Gilmary Shea, *History of the Catholic Church in the United States* (New York, 1892), IV, 709.

That he soon became aware of his nomination is now certain and explains his hasty retreat to Europe to avoid the appointment. At the earliest opportunity he set out for the continent and, as one historian notes, "came to Spain in the autumn of 1852 in order to escape being made Bishop of Monterey, California."[68]

FUGE AB EPISCOPO TAMQUAM A PECCATO

Before leaving Philadelphia, Father Amat wrote to the Superior General and pleaded with him to have the nomination suppressed.[69] There is no indication, however, that the General took any action along these lines although he did approve Amat's transfer to Madrid as Rector of the Community's Novitiate.[70] This is also confirmed in a letter of the Reverend Jose Escarra written from Madrid on September 6, 1852 announcing the installation of the Congregation of the Mission in the new house ceded to them by the Government.[71] In any event, by October 9th, Amat had arrived and was deeply immersed in the routines of his new position.[72]

The Holy See has a persistency in some matters that borders the phenomenal. Amat was sought out in Spain by Propaganda Fide. The reluctant candidate again appealed to the General and this time the matter was discussed in the council meeting for May 30, 1853. It was proposed that

[68]Benito Paradela, C.M., op. cit., p. 158.

[69]Archives of Saint Mary's Seminary (hereafter referred to as ASMS), Amat to Superior General, Philadelphia, May 20, 1852.

[70]In less than thirty years, the Congregation of the Mission in the United States saw five of its priests raised to the episcopacy. Pius IX was once heard to remark to a complaining Superior General, "It is for you to plant the garden, for me to pluck the flowers."

[71]AMM, "Registre . . .," II, 67.

[72]AJMM, An unidentified note reads "1852, 9 Octubre, llega a Madrid el Sr. Amat." Cf. also Registre . . .," II, 81 (December 27, 1852).

Amat be named superior and director of the Daughters of Charity in Chile[73] and on October 22nd *"sale de Madrid el Sr. Amat para Chile."*[74] This last move harmonizes with a note from Archbishop Joseph Sadoc Alemany which mentioned that "as soon as he heard of his appointment, he withdrew from Philadelphia to Spain and thereafter passed on to France for the purpose of taking passage to Chile and so to hide himself."[75]

But by this time the bulls of appointment had already been issued.[76] When this news reached him, Amat wrote directly to the Prefect of the Sacred Congregation of Propaganda Fide:

> I am greatly distressed because of my lack of knowledge, holiness and prudence and for these reasons I left Philadelphia last year. Knowing full well my lack of qualifications I think God in His infinite mercy has called me to the Congregation of the Mission that I might lead a religious life and lacking the helps of this life I fear I might lose my soul. Therefore, I pray you to allow me to remain in my obscure place in the community. . . .[77]

One final communication to Cardinal Fransoni was sent early the next month after having received the bulls:

> The letters ordering my submission to the burden of the episcopate have been received by our Father General who has left the ultimate choice to me in this matter. I still think I should decline because it is a threat to my salvation. But fearing that the judgment may be an effect of my weakness and fearing lest I resist the will of God . . . I sought advice from my spiritual director and had many Masses offered to find out

[73]AMM, "'Registre . . .," II, 93.

[74]*Annales Espana* (Madrid, 1854), sig. 52.

[75]Santa Barbara Mission Archives (hereafter referred to as SBMA), III, 26. Joseph S. Alemany to Gonzales Rubio, San Francisco, November 29, 1853.

[76]The Bulls were dated July 29, 1853.

[77]Archives of the Sacred Congregation of Propaganda Fide (hereafter referred to as APF), Thaddeus Amat to Cardinal Fransoni, Paris, September 6, 1853.

God's will. All these have convinced me that I should not accept the burden. Therefore, I plead with you to tell His Holiness to relieve me.[87]

News of Amat's reluctance even found its way to California. The Archbishop of San Francisco penned an interesting note to his Vicar in the southland:

The new Bishop of Monterey is the Rt. Rev. Thaddeus Amat of Barcelona, a Father of the Congregation of Saint Vincent de Paul, a man, I am assured, very distinguished for his humility and learning . . . . The Propaganda is trying to forward the Bulls to him. It is to be feared that he will decline and thus there will be another delay of some additional months.[79]

In spite of his personal wishes, Amat was eventually obliged to acquiesce to what he termed the "relentless insistence"[80] of the Holy Father, for when Pius IX was apprised of Amat's refusal, he had the following note sent to the unwilling candidate:

The Holy Father, by virtue of the Apostolic Letter of July 29th of this year, which we enclose, has chosen you to be the Bishop of Monterey in Upper California. And even though you have signified your wish to put aside this appointment, the Moderators of the Institute desire that you proceed to carry out the appointment at once. All these things having been accurately set forth. His Holiness has decided not to revoke the decree and has declared it to be His will that you submit to the office which, therefore, it behooves you to undertake as soon as possible.[81]

And so, bowing before the wishes of the Holy Father, Amat

[78]*Ibid.,* October 3, 1853.

[79]SBMA, III, 26. Joseph S. Alemany to Gonzales Rubio, San Francisco, November 29, 1853.

[80]Archives of the Archdiocese of San Francisco (hereafter referred to as AASF), "*Liber G. Diocesis Sancti Francisci,*" fol. 8, Cardinal Fransoni to Joseph S. Alemany, Rome. n.d.

[81]SBMA, III, 19. Papal Bull, Rome, July 29, 1853.

agreed to the "commission that I took every possible means to avoid."

The date of the consecration was set for January 1st; but it had to be delayed twice because of the poor health of Cardinal Fransoni, "who," as Amat said, "reserved to himself the honor of placing the mitre on this unworthy head."[82] When March 12th was selected for the occasion, Amat wrote out in long-hand a few invitations to his personal friends then at Rome:

> The Bishop-elect of Monterey, T. Amat has the honor of announcing to Dr. Kirby that his consecration will take place next Sunday, second of Lent. His Eminence, the Cardinal Fransoni will perform the ceremony at 8 o'clock in the morning in the Church of the Propaganda.[83]

EPISCOPAL CONSECRATION

It was an impressive event and a large number of Roman prelates and clergy gathered at the Propaganda Fide building on the Piazza di Spagna for the ageless pageant. Bernini's graceful chapel, built for Urban VIII, was elaborately decorated for the occasion with freshly cut flowers. In the same surroundings where Oliver Plunkett and John Henry Newman prepared for their ministry, the consecration ceremony unfolded with liturgical exactitude. Music was provided by the choir of the Urban College. The aging Cardinal Fransoni was assisted by Lettorio Turchi, Bishop of Citta de Castello and William Keane, Bishop of Ross in Ireland.

At the conclusion of the *Te Deum* of thanksgiving, Bishop Thaddeus Amat in mitre and with pastoral staff bestowed his first solemn blessing upon the congregation and

---

[82]APF, Thaddeus Amat to Propaganda, Rome, February 3, 1854.

[83]Archives of Pontificio Collegio Irlandese, Thaddeus Amat to Dr. Kirby, Rome, March 10, 1854.

then made his obeisance *ad multos annos* at the feet of the consecrator and concluded the ceremonies of the Mass and of the consecration by reading the last Gospel of Saint John.[84]

As the new bishop moved slowly down the aisle, all were eager to catch a glimpse of the newly consecrated Ordinary of Monterey in whom there could be seen the dignified and manly countenance which already bore the impress of that forceful character which marked him throughout his entire life.

With the exhortation to "Pray for your bishop that the burden he was reluctant to accept, he may not be reluctant to bear,"[85] Thaddeus Amat began an episcopate that would be as plentiful in results as it was extensive in years. His first pastoral letter, penned in classical latin grammer, expressed his hopes and prayers for the California apostolate that lay ahead. Replete with copious references to Sacred Scripture and the Fathers, the letter was, nonetheless, couched in the simple terms of expression which were Amat's hallmark. The final sentence asked for the special intercession of the Blessed Virgin, Star of the Sea, that he might have a successful voyage to California and that his ministry might be worthy and fruitful. As was usual in those written from Rome, the pastoral was dated "from without the Flaminian Gate" recalling the now famous letter of Cardinal Wiseman which, in 1850, had stirred so much of a no-popery outcry in England. Emblazoned on the front page of Amat's first message to his people was the freshly designed coat-of-arms of the new Bishop of Monterey.

---

[84] Cf. the *Giornale di Roma* for March 13, 1854 for an account of the ceremony.

[85] SBMA, III, 34. Thaddeus Amat to the Faithful, Rome, March 12, 1854.

A few days after his consecration on March 18th, Amat was received in private audience by Pope Pius IX. The Holy Father anxiously asked about the status of the Church in California only to find that its bishop knew less about it than himself. This much he did know, his chief problem would be a shortage of clergy and to this the pope indicated that every attempt would be made to secure clerical personnel from Sale-Brignon College in Genoa, a seminary operated under the auspices of the Sacred Congregation of Propaganda Fide. In addition, Pius pledged the financial assistance of Propagation de la Foi, both in Paris and Lyons. The audience was terminated after almost an hour during which the pontiff re-affirmed his intentions to remain actively aware of the destinies of the California Church. It must have been a memorable day for both the pope and his Bishop of Monterey. Both men were exceptionally great characters and both were destined to leave lasting impressions in their spheres of endeavor, one on the world at large, the other on a small missionary diocese.

Before departing from the Eternal City, Amat also made the customary visits to the ranking cardinals of the curia and members of the diplomatic corps. Everyone he left a little poorer from the encounter for he had absolutely no hesitation in making his needs known whether it be for personnel or for financial assistance.

With his business concluded, he left Rome on March 30th[86] for his native Spain where he had an exhausting schedule pre-arranged for pleading his cause to Catalonia. While in Barcelona, he was authorized by that city's ordinary to preach in numerous churches regarding the desolate condition of Catholicism in the Western United States. He was given lodging at the home of a long-time friend,

[86]*Giornale di Roma,* April 3, 1854.

Domingo Alaban at No. 30 Rambla de San Jose.[87] The local journals note that the day after his arrival by rail, on April 18th, Amat

> . . . dijo Misa en la parroquia del Pino, en cual fue bautizado. El respetabilisimo señor cura parroco de dicha parroquia de obsequio con todas las consideraciones debidas de los Apostoles. . . .[88]

Amat was no less cordially received by other pastors in Barcelona and the indefatigable bishop preached endlessly on the need for vocations, assuring the young people they would be eagerly welcomed in the United States where, as he said, "the bishops are well disposed."[89] The visit to the city of his birth was over all too soon, but the days spent at Barcelona were obviously fruitful ones for we are told that

> De regreso a su Diocesis recluto en Barcelona a varios jovenes deseosos de consagrarse a las misiones extranjeras.[90]

Near the end of the month, Amat went on to Madrid where he again extolled the needs of the missions.[91] A formal reception there by his former confreres must have awakened his earlier wishes to remain there "hidden away" from the yoke of the episcopate but, always the realist, Amat spent little time on "could-have-beens" and centered all his attention on the work at hand.

The grueling schedule Amat set for himself in Spain was followed throughout the greater part of Europe and accounts for the delay of more than a year and a half before

[87]AALA, Thaddeus Amat to n.n., Barcelona, April 26, 1854. On the back of this letter, Amat notes that he was staying at the address given in the text. A visit by this author to that area revealed that, on at least three occasions since the turn of the century, the titles and numbers of the streets have undergone change. Hence it was impossible to locate the exact residence.

[88]El Ancora de Barcelona, April 20, 1854.

[89]ASMS, 325-8544.26, Thaddeus Amat to n.n., Barcelona, April 26, 1854.

[90]Jose Herrera, C.M., op. cit., p. 434.

[91]Archives of the Archdiocese of Toledo, Miscellaneous Book of Patentes, p. 492.

he finally arrived in his new diocese. He returned to Rome late in June of 1854 to complete preparations for the removal of Saint Vibiana's relics to Monterey and during the following months criss-crossed Italy and France echoing his pleas. He was welcomed in Paris at the Vincentian motherhouse early in 1855 and used the old Hotel des Lorges as the base of his many mission journeys. On May 7th, he wrote to one of his confreres that,

> I have the satisfaction of writing to you on the eve of leaving for Ireland for a few days. . . . On the 19th of this month, with the help of God, I shall leave Havre.[92]

Accompanying the bishop on his second voyage across the seas to America were four novices, three postulants and the three "clergymen"[93] upon whom Amat had conferred Tonsure and the Minor Orders two days earlier at Paris. Instead of sailing to New Orleans as previously planned, the bishop decided to go directly to New York so as to leave the nuns at nearby Emmitsburg for their "Americanization" training.

The ocean voyage seems to have been routine enough and the party arrived in the United States within three weeks and, after what was surely an enlightening visit with New York's archbishop, Amat went on to Philadelphia where he was greeted enthusiastically by Bishop John Neumann[94] and the host of friends he had acquired in the "freedom city." From there he went to Emmitsburg and then on to Baltimore where he was the guest of Archbishop Francis Patrick Kenrick, also a friend from his Philadelphia days. The two prelates discussed at great length the problems facing the American Church and agreed to exchange

[92]AALA, Thaddeus Amat to Francis Burlando, Paris, May 7, 1855.

[93]*Viz.,* Benito Capdevila, Cypriano Rubio and Francis Mora.

[94]AALA, Thaddeus Amat to Francis Burlando, Pittsburg, June 24, 1855.

views in later years by mail. Amat's visit was prominently noted by the local press:

The Rt. Rev. Dr. Amat, Bishop of Monterey, arrived in this city some days ago, on his return from Spain, where much of his time has been engaged since his appointment to this new See. On Sunday last, the Rt. Rev. Prelate was in Emmitsburg. At the Church attached to Saint Joseph's Academy, he confirmed thirty of the young ladies of the Academy and on the same day thirty-nine persons at Saint Joseph's Church in this town.[95]

From the premier see, Amat journeyed to Emmitsburg where he picked up the newly professed Spanish nuns along with three others provided by the Daughters of Charity for the California mission. Then on to Perryville, the scene of many of his earlier years in the states. In the small town itself he administered Confirmation to 163 children and preached on the mercy of God and the need for prayer. Then he proceeded on to Saint Louis where he wrote:

Informed of the destitute state of my diocese . . . I directed my views to establish in Monterey the Sisters of Charity, to take care of all the unfortunate human beings many of whom found their misery where they expected to find plenty of gold.[96]

By mid October, Amat and his travelling companions were back in New York and on the 20th they sailed for Aspinwall or Colon City on Limon Bay in north central Panama. Their voyage to the isthmus was remarkably calm and there was "not even a white cap on the waters."[97] Transferring to the Pacific Mail Company's steamship, *John C. Stephens*, the party left Panama on November 1st

[95]The *Leader*, June 23, 1855.

[96]*Ibid.*, July 21, 1855. A letter written to the Editor from Saint Vincent's Church in Saint Louis.

[97]AALA, n.n. to Charles Conroy, Saint Joseph, Missouri, September 17, 1951.

and after a two week cruise the ship reached her wharf in San Francisco safely.[98] Amat's arrival being unexpected, there was no formal welcoming ceremony at the time beyond that usually reserved for the docking of such a large ship.[99] Immediately after docking, the bishop proceeded to the house of Archbishop Joseph Sadoc Alemany[100] whose acquaintance he had first made at the Seventh Provincial Council of Baltimore in 1849.

[98]New York *Freeman's Journal and Catholic Register*, December 22, 1855.

[99]There were 944 passengers on the ship.

[100]AASF, *Liber Visitationis Episcopalis Diocesis Sancti Francisci*, p. 12, entry for November 14, 1855.

CHAPTER TWO

BISHOP OF MONTEREY

THE HISTORY of the Catholic Church in the State of California dates from the explorations of Juan Rodriguez Cabrillo in 1542 and Sebastian Vizcaino in 1602. These men, representing a Catholic Power, were accompanied by priests who conducted divine service on these shores over three centuries ago. In a more proximate and particular sense, the narrative begins with the establishment, by Padre Junipero Serra, of Mission San Diego de Alcala on July 16, 1769. The story of the California Missions, built and cared for by the Franciscan Fathers, is an epic of the west. From the beginning in 1769 until the erection of San Francisco Solano, in the present Sonoma County, twenty one of these establishments were founded. There the Indians learned the techniques of agriculture and rude manufacture. The story of the Missions has, in fact, unique interest and this phase of our ecclesiastical history has been described by the pens of Zephyrin Engelhardt, O.F.M., and his successor, the scholarly Maynard J. Geiger, O.F.M. In their many volumes, the well documented account of those eighty years which saw the rise, prosperity, and ruin of the outposts of Christian civilization in the valleys and on the shoreline of California is prosaicly and historically narrated.

The decline of the Missions was rapid, resulting as it did from "secularization," the legal process which took away the mission establishments from the authority of the Franciscan friars. In 1834 a plan was inaugurated and carried out by the authorities in California for the temporal welfare and spiritual interests of the Indians. Lands and herds were expropriated by private parties, and even the churches were sold or leased without sanction of law and justice.

So far had the ruin proceeded that, in 1840 the desperate plea made by the padres for help was answered. Through a formal resolution of the Mexican Congress enacted four years earlier, the Diocese of Both Californias was established. Unfortunately the newly-appointed bishop, Fray Francisco Garcia Diego y Moreno, O.F.M., was almost powerless due to the government's failure to entrust the Pious Fund to his care. He did, however, succeed in erecting a seminary at Santa Ines, on a tract of land granted to him by Governor Manuel Micheltorena. Worn out by his efforts to better conditions in the Californias, the bishop died at Santa Barbara on April 30, 1846, at the age of sixty, whereupon the administration of the vast diocese passed into the hands of Father Francisco Gonzales Rubio, O.F.M., who for the next four and a half years acted as vicar-capitular. He saw great changes in the life and fortunes of California in that comparatively brief period. Gonzales Rubio had hardly taken his new office, when war broke out between Mexico and the United States. The struggle in California resulted in the raising of the American flag at Monterey on July 7th, 1846. With that act a new chapter of history began, and the part which the Catholic Church has since played has been nothing less than phenomenal.

In 1848, an epochal event brought about the beginning of a new era in the economic and political character of Alta California and greatly altered its historic future. This event was of course, the discovery of gold at Coloma, near the site of the present city of Sacramento. Excitement produced by the news spread to the remotest hamlets of the country and even to foreign lands. With the resulting influx of fortune-seekers and adventurers, the population of Alta California in two years exceeded 100,000 and continued to grow by leaps and bounds. This presented an unexpected and very perplexing problem for Father Rubio for although the newcomers were of all classes and creeds, not a few of their number were Catholics. The handful of priests in the land was incapable of ministering to the spiritual needs of so many people. In northern and central California, mining towns sprung up overnight and while the southern districts were left unaffected for a time even that area needed more attention than it was receiving by the Church.

June of 1850 saw a new bishop consecrated for California in the person of Joseph Sadoc Alemany, O.P. Alemany had been a missionary to scattered groups of Catholics in the rural districts of the east and early midwest. He spoke English well, and had an equal fluency in several other languages. His arrival in the Golden State came shortly after its admission to the Union. With excellent executive ability, the new bishop set himself to the formidable tasks then facing the Church in California. Father Gonzalez Rubio had secured the services of several religious orders. and Alemany proceeded to build upon the foundations laid by his Franciscan predecessor. One of the first permanent results of Alemany's plans was the establishment by the Jesuit Fathers, in 1851, of Santa Clara College. A few years later Saint Ignatius' College opened its doors in San Francisco. Several communities of Sisters arrived in California to establish orphanages and academies for girls. To this period can also be traced the earliest plans for the erection of the hospitals, sorely needed in the new and rapidly developing State.

Some important jurisdictional changes affected Bishop Alemany's activities. The peninsula of Baja California was cut off from the old Diocese of Monterey since the Holy See recognized the different complexities of the two nations. The southern part of the state, notwithstanding a significant migration of Americans over the old trails, remained predominately Spanish in speech. Indians scattered through the deserts and the mountains were, on occasion, inclined to be unruly. A partial answer to the questions posed by these and other matters seemed to demand a readjustment of diocesan authority in an effort to reduce the handicaps brought on by distance and poor communications. On July 29, 1853, the Diocese of Monterey was divided. A new see of provincial rank was established and Bishop Alemany was transferred to San Francisco as Metropolitan Archbishop.

The new archbishop now devoted all his energies to the complex and difficult problems which had been created for the Church in the northern half of the state. A fair percentage of the gold seekers were Catholic, coming as they did from many areas. Although many of the newcomers hailed from the eastern seaboard there were others not familiar with the English language and it thus became necessary to provide priests who could minister to those people whose mother tongue was not English. Another problem was the erection of churches in the new mining towns. Costs of building were high, and even a modest structure represented a considerable outlay of money. The settlements were not always permanent, since prosperity depended entirely upon the fortunes of mining. Hence, care had to be taken that expenditures were used in the most efficient manner. It is not surprising that sometimes fairly commodious churches were erected in towns which later declined in population and influence. All religious bodies had this same problem to some extent but it affected Catholic parish organization more considerably than others.

In the course of time these difficulties were overcome and by degrees, permanent centers of population developed, some of them destined to see rapid growth. San Francisco itself had a population of about 34,000 according to the special census of 1852. Next largest of California's cities was Sacramento, at that time in the Archdiocese of San Francisco. San Jose, in the Santa Clara Valley, was taking on some importance and another considerable town was growing up at Stockton. The beginnings of many of the prosperous cities now dotting the eastern shore of the Bay of San Francisco held out promise for the future.

ON THE SCENE

Amat's first "briefing session" on the California Church probably came during his interview with Archbishop Hughes in New York. Late in 1848 Hughes had been delegated to submit a report on the problems of California Catholicity to the Seventh Provincial Council of Baltimore and at that time had sought the advice of Don Jose de la Guerra y Noriega, a prominent resident of Santa Barbara. De la Guerra's reply was as extensive as it was accurate. He calculated the number of Catholics in the state before the gold discovery at about twenty-five or thirty thousand. He estimated the number of Christian Indians at between ten to fifteen thousand but hazarded no views on the Gentile tribes. The clergy consisted of four secular priests, four extern priests, one Dominican and seven Franciscans. Comments on the condition of the old missions and other church property was treated as well as the controverted "Pious Fund of the Californias." De la Guerra heartily endorsed Hughes' proposal that the new bishop be selected from among the "several Spanish priests" then available.

> As to what you add, that it ought to be occupied by a Spanish ish priest, I judge that to be fitting, because the Catholics of this country are almost all Spanish-American, with whom the Spaniards are in sympathy.[1]

The appointment of Joseph Sadoc Alemany to the Diocese of Monterey had been a great satisfaction to California's Catholic population and with his advancement to the Provincial Seat at San Francisco, the old Diocese of Monterey was no less anxious than before to see a Spaniard wearing the mitre in their midst.

With Amat's arrival in California in late 1855, the state's two prelates began a series of meetings at Alemany's residence near the cathedral, a residence so poor as to evoke the comment from Herbert Vaughn that "no man is more poorly lodged in the whole city"[2] than the archbishop. Nor did Amat think the less of a man who lived in such unpretentious surroundings for he was quick to perceive that the Church in California was lacking much of what easterners, and certainly Europeans, thought to be routine appurtenances.

[1]SBMA, Quoted in Joseph A. Thompson, O.F.M., *El Gran Capitan* (Los Angeles, 1961), p. 221-222.
[2]*The Dublin Review,* VI (New Series) (January-April, 1856), 28.

Considering his previous experience, it is not surprising to find that Bishop Amat was not too well briefed on the problems about to confront him. Certainly he knew of the more pressing needs, for even if he did not participate in the discussions at Baltimore some years earlier, his conversations with officials at Propaganda Fide in Rome and those of Propagation de la Foi in Paris and Lyons, as well as his long chats with Archbishops Hughes and Kenrick gave him some insight into the problems that laid ahead. Alemany had this to say just a few months earlier in one of his routine reports on the Diocese of Monterey:

> This Diocese of Monterey in California, probably has not so many pressing wants (as San Francisco) for the great mass of immigrants settle north of that Diocese. But as its population is much dispersed, and it has been accustomed to pay but very little for the support of Church and clergy, it is difficult to make progress, and even to secure a sufficient number of clergymen without your aid. Hence several churches have no priests; the good Dominican Sisters of Monterey are yet in debt for their Academy. Some of the old churches will be greatly injured by the rains for want of funds to repair them. Many seminarians have arrived and several more are expected to arrive soon, and if your charitable work for the propagation of Faith can make a good appropriation for that Diocese, the new Bishop, Dr. Amat or myself when he comes, will be enabled to relieve greatly the churches of that Diocese from their great necessities.[3]

To be sure, California had changed greatly during the years since Bishop Francisco Garcia Diego y Moreno first carried the crozier in the early 1840's for the American occupation had altered forever the course of the area's development and the rush of gold seekers after 1849 brought a flood of newcomers who made the problems of the Church all the more acute.

[3]APF, Joseph S. Alemany to Propaganda Fide, San Francisco, n.d.

The Southern California that faced Thaddeus Amat was composed of the so-called "cow counties" designated thusly not in derision, but because the sobriquet actually described their chief source of wealth, cattle raising. There were horticultural interests too, orchards and vineyards. But everything depended on rainfall, which was as inadequate as it was unpredictable. In this land of ranches and ranchos, the population would increase quite slowly and the people would remain mostly Spanish-speaking, isolated as they were from outside influences. Fewer than a score of priests served the few churches that had outlived the ruins of the missions but from this meagre clergy would come a greatness that mere numbers could never attain.

Several contemporary accounts reveal the state of the Church, none more graphically than the one by Doctor Gregory Phelan:

> This State is Catholic at heart; its history and traditions and reminiscences are inseparably connected with the Church and her ministers. And shall we not hope that its future will be Catholic—that its enterprising population will profess the true faith, and that commissioned teachers may everywhere be found comforting the afflicted, instructing the ignorant, and enlightening those in error or in doubt. Time, and the grasping hand of Mexican officials, followed by American utilitarian progress and improvement, and but too often by acts of vandalism on the part of our enlightened countrymen, have not yet effaced the evidences of the labor and zeal of the Franciscan missionaries who first planted Christianity and civilization upon these shores. Let the work go on. The field has widened and become vastly more important. A few years ago, the Missionary labored to implant the great truths of Christianity in the untutored mind of the poor savage, and at the same time sought to draw him forth from his miserable habitation (which was nothing more than an excavation in the earth, covered with branches and other material) to teach him the arts and duties of civilized life. Large churches, comfortable

dwellings, commodious workshops, herds of cattle, fields of grain, vineyards, orchards, etc., were part of the fruits of their labors. I need not speak of the spiritual blessings showered upon them. But a change, sad in many respects, came o'er the scene. Since the Golden Era of California, a majority of those who came in search of the precious metal, were not Catholics. The vast immigration was composed of the bold, enterprising youth of every race and creed and country. It is true there was a mixture of the vicious with the good. Convicts, desperadoes, and others, who deserted from vessels and got here by various means, have, by their lawless acts, cast a foul stain upon our young State that will require years to wipe away. There are good and bad in every community, and this is no exception. Still I believe our character abroad is below what justice requires. I will venture to assert that in proportion to her population, California possesses the most active, bold, energetic, and educated people in the world. There are some illiterate persons from the Western States and other places; but nearly all who come from the Eastern States, and the number of thousands have received a common school education, and not a few from other portions of the Union, have received literary instruction, to a greater or less extent. Many are graduates, and some are distinguished in the learned professions.

There are Catholics scattered in every town and village—upon every mountain and valley. Many have grown careless and indifferent—some are in districts rarely visited by a Priest, having but few opportunities to perform their religious duties, and many obstacles in their path. Such is the field of our Missionaries—a people whose conversion would be a great triumph to the Church, as well as an inestimable blessing to the recipient of the graces and consolations following their conversion. A great deal has been done by our devoted and self-sacrificing Prelate and his zealous assistants, and, no doubt, in a short time the wants of the people will be supplied, and the harvest will yield a hundred fold.[4]

Another observation, surely noted by Amat, was the peculiar shape of his new jurisdiction. As it had been di-

[4]New York *Freeman's Journal and Catholic Register*, December 22, 1855.

vided, the Diocese of Monterey was anything but an attractive area from a material point of view. And Archbishop Alemany's comment that "I should have preferred the smaller labor of Monterey" seems a bit exaggerated in view of the manner in which he had the province divided. A line had been drawn at 37 degrees and five minutes, thus securing for the Archdiocese of San Francisco all the major towns, mining districts and railroads in the state. Possibly as much as 92% of California's population was thus retained in the archdiocese, leaving for Monterey not so much as a respectable-sized town in the entire diocese. About the only advantageous aspect of the southern jurisdiction was the vast coastal ranchos and even these, by their very size, tended to prevent the growth of population centers. Amat found himself with 75,984 square miles in an area where less than a score of priests served the few churches that had outlived the ruin of the missions.

PROSINT

Before leaving Rome, Bishop Amat had been entrusted by the Sacred Congregation of the Consistory with the pallium for San Francisco's new archbishop. And even though Alemany had been authorized to function as metropolitan without that symbol of his office, it was decided to have the investiture ceremonies as soon as possible. The colorful function, first of its kind ever witnessed in California, was set for November 18[5] and was described in these words:

> Saint Mary's Cathedral was yesterday the scene of an exceedingly impressive and very dignified ceremonial. The pallium, or token of archiepiscopal rank, which was recently brought from Rome by Dr. Amat, Bishop of Monterey, was conferred

[5]APF, Thaddeus Amat to Cardinal Barnabo, San Francisco, January 18, 1856.

upon Archbishop Allemany [sic] of this city. . . . A grand
Pontifical Mass was celebrated by the Bishop of Monterey who
preached a very eloquent and suitable sermon on the occasion.[6]

The large area of the cathedral, its galleries and even the
vestibules were jammed with an attentive congregation.
The Solemn Pontifical Mass was followed by the investiture of the humeral and pectoral pendant for the first time
made the people "aware of the organization of the Catholic Church in California."[7]

Soon after the ceremonies, Amat and the archbishop set
out for Monterey where, as it was said, "the climate and
quality of the soil resembled Castille." On November 25
the bishop arrived in his see city, where he was to take
formal canonical possession of the diocese bearing the
name of the old California capital.[8] Then, as today, Monterey was a picturesque town, lying on the sloping shores
at the southern end of a bay, within the northern curve
of Point Pinos, which protects the harbor from heavy
seas and winds. The archbishop installed Monterey's new
bishop at San Carlos Presidio Chapel which had served as
the pro-cathedral of the diocese.[9] It was a modest, almost
private affair, performed chiefly to satisfy canonical re-
quirements. Amat had no intention of staying at Monterey
permanently and for the time being planned to make Santa
Barbara the temporary center of his activities. After a short

[6]*Catholic Telegraph and Advocate,* December 29, 1855.

[7]Thomas Denis McSweeney, *Cathedral on California Street* (Fresno, 1952),
p. 37.

[8]Thaddeus Amat, C.M., *Exhortacion Pastoral* (Los Angeles, 1856), p. 4.

[9]Interestingly enough, Archbishop Alemany appointed Amat Vicar General of
the Archdiocese of San Francisco on November 23, 1855, a position that he most
probably occupied for the next quarter century. The author stumbled across a note
to this effect in the Archives of the Archdiocese of San Francisco, *"Liber A, Diocesis Sancti Francisci in California Superioribus,"* H-5, Fol. 15.

visit in Monterey,[10] he left for Santa Barbara where he arrived on December 2. Two days later, on the patronal feast of the city, he was conducted with great solemnity by clergy and people to the old mission church, where he celebrated pontifical Mass. Archbishop Alemany had recommended Santa Barbara for the bishop's residence because of its relative accessibility to the far corners of the vast diocese. Among the functions presided over by Bishop Amat in his early days in the Channel City was the solemn ceremony of installing the remains of Saint Vibiana in Our Lady of Sorrows Church.[11]

After several days of conferences with the Very Reverend Gonzales Rubio, O.F.M., who had been administering the diocese, the bishop went to Los Angeles where he was enthusiastically welcomed by the populace. His arrival was chronicled in the *Southern Californian*:

> Bishop Amat of Monterey arrived in Los Angeles on the 15th of December. An immense multitude of people, with the Catholic priest, were waiting to receive him at the west end of town, where he left his carriage, and walked, dressed in full canonicals, to the Church, dispensing benedictions as he went along. On entering the Church, after the usual ceremonies at the altar, he ascended the pulpit, and made an eloquent address to his hearers in Spanish and English. The Catholic portion of Los Angeles appear to be delighted with their bishop. He has invited the people to a meeting, for the purpose of taking measures to establish a college and also to provide for a settlement at Los Angeles of the Sisters of Char-

[10]In the Mexican period, the capital had been shifted from Monterey to San Diego, Santa Barbara, or Los Angeles at the caprice of the governors. At the beginning of the American period, the military governors stationed themselves at Monterey. But the sudden importance of the mining areas seemed to dictate a more centrally located point and in 1854 the legislature designated Sacramento as the capital of the state.

[11]Santa Barbara *Gazette*, December 6, 1855.

ity. He has been administering the Sacrament of Confirmation to great numbers of Catholic youth.[12]

It was the third time that the sleepy little pueblo of Los Angeles had welcomed a Catholic bishop, the first having been that of Francisco Garcia Diego y Moreno in March, 1843, and the second that of Joseph Sadoc Alemany in September, 1851. Among those witnessing the arrival of Amat at Los Angeles was Edmond Venisse, a Picpus Father from the Sandwich Islands. According to his account, Amat's

> entrance was solemn, full of spirit and gladness. While the ringing of the bells filled the air the Indians dressed in their gorgeous costumes, mingled with ranchers who had come from distant parts, crowded into the streets and formed a joyous throng, lively yet recollected: at the approach of the bishop all knelt with respect to receive the blessing.[13]

There is no record of the bishop's reactions to this welcome but he must have been greatly impressed by the city that one day would be his home. However, the Los Angeles that greeted Thaddeus Amat in 1855 was little more than a struggling pueblo. California had long been a pawn in Mexican politics, torn as it was by civil war between the Californians themselves and the few American inhabitants who joined sides in various revolutions. One chronicler wisely noted that

> Los Angeles County and the pueblo were a political football for years. The war between the United States and Mexico and the efforts of America to wrest California from Mexico kept the countryside in a state of general suspense.[14]

[12]December 22, 1855.

[13]*Annals de la Propagation de la Foi* (1858), p. 67. Translated from the French by Brother V. Edmund, F.S.C. The letter was written from Copiapo, Chile on June 20, 1856.

[14]Boyle Workman, *The City That Grew* (Los Angeles, 1936), p. 16.

And there is ample evidence that this suspense lasted on for a full decade after California's entry into the Union.

With the location of the sisters and other items of business attended to, Bishop Amat journeyed south as far as San Diego before returning to Santa Barbara where he established himself at the old mission. Among the first matters on his agenda were plans for a seminary where candidates could be trained for the diocesan priesthood.[15] California's first seminary, established by Bishop Garcia Diego at Santa Ines, had never functioned satisfactorily and Bishop Amat thought it preferable to keep his seminarians at Santa Barbara until a more suitable arrangement could be worked out.[16] The Reverend Blasius Raho, C.M., who had accompanied Amat to Californa, was appointed superior of the seminary which the bishop set up in his own home and here under Raho's direction the three students from Spain continued their studies.

Among other appointments of Amat's was the designation of Father Gonzalez Rubio, O.F.M., as vicar general of the diocese,[17] a post he had occupied under the former ordinary. The Reverend Anacletus Lestrade, C.SS.CC. of Los Angeles was named vicar forane for the southern part of the unwieldy diocese and later in the summer, Raho was delegated vicar general *a latere* for the express purpose of making a visitation of San Gabriel, San Juan Capistrano, San Luis Rey, and San Diego.

---

[15]The Cash Book used by Bishop Amat indicates that he spent $1,395 in 1856 and $2,961 in 1857 for the upkeep of the seminary at Santa Barbara, a considerable outlay for such a struggling diocese.

[16]Finbar Kenneally, O.F.M., *The Catholic Seminaries of California as Educational Institutions* (Toronto, 1956), p. 6.

[17]Archives of the Archdiocese of Los Angeles (hereafter referred to as AALA), "Libro Borrador," p. 26.

The seminarians[18] who had come with the bishop from Spain were given minor orders along with three Franciscans on February 24, 1856; on March 8 all of these advanced to the subdiaconate; and on March 12, four diocesan and one Franciscan were ordained deacons. March 19 was the day selected by the bishop for ordaining the four diocesan candidates and another deacon to the priesthood. The ordinations and the immediate prospect of additional recruits from Europe enabled Bishop Amat to assign pastors to several of the vacant parishes attached to the old missions and to consider the opening of several new ones. This welcome acquisition of five new priests, along with the favorable decision of the United States Land Commission confirming the right of the Church to certain buildings attached to the missions, were a great boon to the infant and struggling diocese.

The apostolic brief, which Bishop Amat had sought from Pius IX in 1854 allowing the celebration *in foro externo* of the feast of Saint Vibiana, was received in March, 1856, and publicly proclaimed at the end of the month,[19] the feast being given the rank of greater double in all the churches of the diocese. Even at this early date rumors about a proposed cathedral for the Diocese of Monterey were rampant despite the fact that there is no extant record of any such plans by Amat. One Santa Barbara paper reported that

> It is the intention of Bishop Amat to commence soon the erection of a cathedral in Santa Barbara, near the site of the present chapel. On the completion of the cathedral the building now used as a chapel will be converted into a nunnery.[20]

[18]*Viz.,* Vincent Llover and Dominic Serrano.

[19]SBMA, III, 84, Decree, Rome, March 28, 1856.

[20]Santa Barbara *Gazette,* May 22, 1856.

When the Picpus Fathers were recalled in the summer of 1856 to their posts in the Sandwich Islands after several decades of their "California exile,"[21] Father Raho was named to the pastorate of the Los Angeles parish and set out at once to redecorate the church. During the fall, this work was undertaken by "the best artist in the city"[22] and was brought to completion early in December. A local historian made this interesting observation on the outcome of the renovation:

> During the administration of Padre Blas Raho, a genial and broad minded Italian, several attempts were made . . . to improve the old church at the Plaza; and in 1861, the historic edifice, so long unchanged, was practically rebuilt. The front adobe wall, which had become damaged by rains, was taken down and reconstructed of brick; some alterations were made in the tower; and the interesting old tiled roof was replaced— to the intense regret of later and more appreciative generations—with modern, less durable shingles.[23]

The work of painting the exterior and redecorating the interior of the building had been a costly enterprise for the times. It was decided, therefore, on the day of the blessing of the church, to begin a subscription for funds and the local newspaper carried this item in a prominent place:

> We hope that all the faithful will contribute, with their customary generosity, in order to replace and regild the gates and to place thereon new ornaments befitting the church.[24]

So generously did the city respond to the plea that by December 21, 1856 the renovated and newly adorned church was solemnly re-dedicated. Amat noticed that the occasion

[21]Reginald Yzendoorn, SS.CC., *History of the Catholic Mission in the Hawaiian Islands* (Honolulu, 1927), p. 187.

[22]*Viz.*, Henrique Penelon.

[23]Harris Newmark, *Sixty Years in Southern California* (New York, 1930), p. 293.

[24]*El Clamor Publico*, December 13, 1856.

had been recorded on the very walls of the edifice with these appropriate words: *Los Fieles de Esta Parroquia a la Reina de Los Angeles.*

Amat was quick to realize that the Los Angeles he had known two years earlier was gradually beginning to dominate the scene in Southern California. Several attempts already had been made to divide the state, one as early as 1850 advocating a separate territory to be known as Central California. A more vigorous attempt came about a year later and in 1859 the state legislature even approved a bill to that end. The counties of San Luis Obispo, Santa Barbara, Los Angeles, San Bernardino and San Diego were to be withdrawn and erected in the Territory of Colorado. Only the controversy over slavery in the United States Congress killed the bill. The bishop perceived that, in any event, Los Angeles would be the logical and geographical center of future Southern California activities. By the summer of 1857 he had made up his mind to ask Rome to transfer the seat of his diocese to Los Angeles. It was also pointed out that the dissension then prevalent in Santa Barbara between himself and the friars would attract less public attention if the administrative center of the diocese were removed to another area.

With the few funds already collected by the Society of Saint Vibiana,[25] Amat provided for the erection of an episcopal residence adjoining the Church of Our Lady of the Angels. No public announcement was made of the plans to make Los Angeles his headquarters but a San Francisco newspaper soon learned of the matter and reported that,

> Bishop Amat will reside at Los Angeles in future. A contract has been made for the construction of parochial buildings.

[25] AALA, Circular, Los Angeles, September 5, 1857. Later known as the Archconfraternity of Saint Vibiana, the society was set up in 1857 to collect funds for a new cathedral.

Upon their completion, they will be occupied by the Bishop. An ecclesiastical seminary is also to be established at Los Angeles.[26]

Although not official, this announcement was much more accurate than many others which appeared from time to time in the press. The parochial buildings mentioned were soon under construction immediately north of the church. The edifice was built of brick, with a long veranda, and served as an ideal episcopal residence. The home continued as the bishop's house and parish residence for the next five decades until the present dwelling of the Claretian Fathers was erected after 1910.

Despite the predominantly Catholic tone of Los Angeles in the 1850's and 1860's, there is reason to believe that Catholicity was something inherited but not practiced by the great majority. Visitors to the city were shocked at its carnival drinking and fighting and, as one author notes, "In a town that took morbid pride in its own sins the forces of morality were slow enough to appear."[27] That isn't to say that there was a total lack of religious practice, however. It was a time of transition and the forces of evil quite naturally attracted the pens of chroniclers. Grassroots devotion to the Blessed Virgin, for instance, remained as one of the chief benefactions from Spanish times. Typical of this devotion to Our Lady of Refuge was a scene reported by one newspaper:

Our native population, assisted by a number of Americans, are making great preparation for the celebration of their great feast. It commences Tuesday, the 8th, it being the *Dia de la Virgin*. The entrances to the Plaza are now being closed up, preparatory to the "Grand Bull Fight." High Mass will be

[26]San Francisco *Bulletin*, June 14, 1858.
[27]Remi Nadeau, *Los Angeles From Mission to Modern City* (New York, 1960), p. 43.

celebrated in the Church on Tuesday morning, and dancing and other rational amusements will be kept up during the remainder of the week.[28]

Religious functions closer to home were also common as is evident from one report in 1858:

Corpus Christi, June 3rd, was quite extensively observed in our town as a holiday. Low and High Masses were said in the Church under the direction of Bishop Amat, with three or four priests assisting in the morning; in the afternoon, both the holy and profane, clergy and laity, together with the school of the Sisters of Charity, nearly a hundred girls, dressed in white, marched in a grand procession around the plaza, escorted by the Southern Rifles and the Lancers, preceded by a band of music. The exact significance of some of the ceremonies I was not able to see into. The musical exercises in the church were, in general, really commendable.[29]

Transferal of the diocesan seat to Los Angeles was only one of many matters Amat wished to discuss with officials at Propaganda Fide. And since correspondence by mail was as slow as it was ineffectual, the bishop decided to go personally to the Eternal City. Father Blasius Raho was named Vicar General[30] and during Amat's absence was given the exceedingly broad jurisdictional powers, granted a few months earlier for just such a need.[31] Amat went first to San Francisco on September 25th and while there conferred several times with Archbishop Alemany about the delicate Franciscan controversy at Santa Barbara. While in the Bay City, the Bishop of Monterey preached several times as noted by the local press:

[28]San Diego *Herald*, December 5, 1857.

[29]The Los Angeles Section of the San Francisco *Bulletin*, June 28, 1858.

[30]Amat had requested the resignation of Father Gonzales Rubio when the latter became superior of the Apostolic College at Santa Barbara. Cf. SBMA, III, 123, Los Angeles, September 24, 1858.

[31]AALA, Propagation de la Foi to Thaddeus Amat, Paris, March 18, 1858.

Solemnity of the Rosary. A grand Pontifical Mass will be celebrated in the Cathedral today at 11 o'clock, it being the anni-
versary of the above solemn festival. Rev. Dr. Amat, Bishop
of Monterey will preach on the occasion.[32]

Shortly thereafter Amat set out for the long and exhausting trip to Rome. He went first to New York and there discussed at length with Archbishop Hughes the feasibility
of opening an American seminary in Europe to train priests
for the United States. When his business had been completed, the bishop set out on October 30th for Europe.[33]

His journey took him first to Paris and the Vincentian motherhouse where he was graciously received by
his confreres after a five-year absence. While in Paris,
Amat wrote several letters ahead to Rome advising the
Prefect of the Propaganda, Cardinal Barnabo,[34] of his im-
pending visit and appraising him of the reasons for his
trip. One of the more perplexing problems facing Amat
was the *bulla cruciata* and its applicability to the Diocese
of Monterey. A rescript received in January, 1856, had allowed him to promulgate the calendar of special feasts
then being used at Baltimore with a few minor exception.[35]
One of California's more prominent clerics had written to
a friend in Ireland of the freedom from certain ecclesiastical laws in his new home. "I don't know whether you are
aware of some of our California liberties. . . . Take, for example, that of eating meat *toties quoties* on every Friday
except the Fridays in Lent. . . ."[36] Amat thought it wise to

---

[32]San Francisco *Call*, October 3, 1858.

[33]SBMA, III, 127, Francisco Caro to Friars, New York, October 29, 1858.

[34]AALA, Thaddeus Amat to Cardinal Barnabo, Paris, December 29, 1858.

[35]*Viz.*, Our Lady of Guadalupe whose feast day was observed on December 12th.

[36]Eugene O'Connell to David Moriarty, San Francisco, June 15, 1853. Quoted
in John Tracy Ellis, *Documents of American Catholic History* (Milwaukee, 1956),
p. 314.

submit the question to Barnabo as to whether he should conform to Baltimore in this matter of fasts and precepts[37] or continue to observe the existing situation.

The bishop arrived in Rome late in March and began at once to dispose of the business matters before him. He wanted to visit Naples where King Francis II had recently succeeded to the throne and then return to Rome sometime after Easter but his actual itinerary is not known. In a letter to Raho, Amat happily announced that "when I come, about September, I will bring with me two priests of the Mission and five Sisters of Charity for the Novitiate." The sisters were a long cherished fulfillment as is obvious in the tone of the letter:

> I shall bring with me likewise, as I am told by Father Sorrentini, it is already agreed upon, 13 or 14 Sisters of San Jose, and they come particularly for the Indians, but they will do whatever think best, though I would like them to become useful to our poor Indians.[38]

On May 28, 1859, Amat wrote again to Father Raho directing that the Litany of the Blessed Virgin was to be recited in all the churches of the diocese either before or after the parish Mass for the intentions of the Holy Father, and especially for the peace of the Church, a step he apparently took in compliance with a desire expressed by the pope in the preceeding April. An interesting note to Archbishop Alemany on June 7 pursued the question of the *bulla cruciata*:

> I received from the Congregation the declaration about the festivals and fasts we are to observe in California (of which I sent you a copy). I inquired in what sense we are to under-

---

[37]In an audience granted on January 23, Pope Pius IX ruled that the old calendar was to continue in force as to feasts and fasts. Regarding abstinence, it was permitted to use the bulla cruciata in the Diocese of Monterey.

[38]AALA, Thaddeus Amat to Blasius Raho, Rome, April 1, 1859.

stand the words about the abstinences *Utatur Bulla Cruciata*: whether it is understood that we can use the privilege of the bull without taking it, as it should be in a country where they are Protestants; or whether it be necessary to interpret it otherwise. The Holy Father answered that we are to conform to the general rule of the fast. For my part I think it is best not to take it, so I abstain from asking for it. If you should think otherwise, I would conform to your views and might ask it for both dioceses.[39]

Amat's reluctance to use the privileges given by Rome were prompted by his own rather severe interpretation of canonical discipline.

Near the end of June, when his business affairs had been for the most part transacted, Bishop Amat departed for Spain and his native Barcelona. It was a pleasant visit and a highly gratifying one for a new spirit of religious zeal was coming alive in Spain and bringing with it some of the former idealism which Amat so greatly admired. He appealed for funds in many familiar churches and everywhere sought clerical recruits especially among the candidates of religious communities. His travels were successful for he had more than enough money to defray his own expenses and those of the others whom he brought back to the United States.

During his absence from Rome, the Sacred Congregation de Propaganda Fide handed down its decision allowing the transfer of his see to Los Angeles where it was said, "considerable numbers [had] settled . . . in the lower part of the country in consequence of the great fertility of climate."[40] The decision was dated July 8, and retained the historic Monterey in the title.[41]

[39]AALA, Thaddeus Amat to Joseph S. Alemany, Rome, June 7, 1859.

[40]William Gleeson, *History of the Catholic Church in California* (San Francisco), II, 269.

[41]AALA, Decretum No. 40, Rome, July 3, 1859.

CHAPTER THREE

THE FRANCISCAN CONTROVERSIES

Ⅾ URING much of Bishop Amat's time in California, there was a notable lack of harmony between the diocesan curia and the Franciscan Fathers at Santa Barbara. It was a period of transition and the difficulties between the two factions are understandable, happening as they did in an era when delineation of ecclesiastical jurisdiction was poorly defined.

Although Monterey had been designated as the city of his residence, Amat never lived there, and he seems to have determined at an early date on Santa Barbara as the center of his diocese. In any event, he took up his residence in February of 1856 at the old mission. The facilities were not very much improved from the previous decade, and this, added to the obvious advantage of having a more centralized location, induced the bishop to propose to the Franciscans that they exchange their foundation[1] in the city for that of the old mission, assuring them he would

---

[1] A new church had been built and dedicated on July 29, 1855 and it became the first parish in Santa Barbara. In fact, it succeeded the functions previously carried out at the Presidio chapel.

grant them the perpetual use[2] of the mission, its adjoining living quarters, a vineyard and two gardens.[3]

The friars were understandably reluctant and replied that Our Lady of Sorrows had been canonically erected as a college and could not be dismembered without explicit permission of the Holy See. Nonetheless, Amat insisted on an immediate transfer, promising to write to Propaganda Fide, giving an explanation both to the pope and to the Franciscan minister general, from whom he received formal approval on July 6. In the meantime, however, the bishop went ahead with the exchange and appointed Father Blasius Raho, C.M., to the pastorate of Our Lady of Sorrows Church. Anxious that the matter be handled discreetly and with as little public knowledge as possible, the bishop advised Father Raho to adhere closely to the schedule of religious functions previously followed by the friars and to fall in with the local customs familiar to the people.

In his subsequent report to Rome,[4] Bishop Amat contended that the friars had been imprudent in their public utterances concerning the loss of their city parish and its transference to diocesan administration, an event which was beginning to have adverse effects on public opinion in Santa Barbara. Amat pointed out that he had assumed the mortgage on the house and had not requested the return of funds already spent by the friars from the accounts of Santa Ines College.[5] It was the bishop's opinion that the exchange was in the best interests of the Franciscans them-

[2]It should be noted that Amat wanted the title to Our Lady of Sorrows Church but wished to grant only the perpetual use of the mission property to the friars, an arrangement that would not seem to have been an adequate *quid pro quo*.

[3]Unfortunately, this property, large though it may have been, was never sufficient to support the friars.

[4]AALA, Thaddeus Amat to Cardinal Barnabo, n.p., April 4, 1859.

[5]AALA, *Ristretto con Sommario* (a document presented to the Sacred Congregation de Propaganda Fide), Paris, February 31, 1860, p. 3.

selves since in his judgment there had been an undue amount of contact between the novices and the laity in their former location. At the mission the young students would be, as he said, "at a healthy distance from the town."[6] Amat obviously considered the transaction a fair one for he pointed out that by canon law he was entitled to designate any church within his diocese as his official residence. However, that the bishop had by no means all responsible parties on his side was evident from the fact that others besides the Franciscans and their friends, notably Archbishop Alemany of San Francisco, contended for many years that the parish should be restored to the friars.

The agent of the United States government for Indian affairs had approached Bishop Amat and asked for several priests to take charge of the natives living around the San Luis Rey area. Knowing something of their history in California and their successes in this highly specialized work, Amat proposed this project to the friars as one worthy of their consideration. The proposal was declined with a show of feeling that intimated a suspicion that the bishop was trying to drive them from the diocese. In their behalf, it must be said, there were only four friars at the mission at this time and even the loss of one would have necessitated the discontinuance of their college, which was both their novitiate and major seminary.

The Catholics of Santa Barbara were becoming increasingly aware of the poor relations between the bishop and the friars, and were inclined to side with the latter. For a century the people had known only the Franciscans and they were quite naturally attached to them. This was not a rare situation since it also existed in parts of Mexico with

[6]*Ibid.*

a similar historical background. One supporter of the Franciscans made this point to the bishop:

> Your Excellency, how can you expect the people to act differently when it is to the Franciscans that we owe what we are in our religion, civil and social life? How can you expect the people to have an equally good opinion of the religious and secular clergy since concerning the first we know from the tradition of our fathers and from our own observations their virtues of every kind. . . .[7]

That all was not harmonious with the people at Santa Barbara is obvious from other sources. One prominent lawyer noted in his diary that

> We have never known such meanness as exists in this settlement. Even the magistrates in the tribunal of Justice cannot be counted upon and the disposition to steal, to cheat, of fraud, of lying, of violence, of intrigue, of abuse, of confidence are most common and prevalent and predominate to an extent that is hard to believe.[8]

Abuses were so extensive that the bishop was forced to forbid midnight Mass at Christmas time because of so many public disorders.[9] The issuance of a pastoral letter by Amat on September 16, 1856, came at the end of a long series of personal pleas on his part and it was obviously aimed at the local populace of Santa Barbara whose abuses were condemned in no uncertain terms. After noting the happiness brought him on his recent parochial visitation, the bishop sadly commented that

> Our joy has been diminished by our observance of the great dangers that threaten and surround us; such as are capable

[7]SBMA, III, 112, Testimony of Pablo de la Guerra, Santa Barbara, 1858.

[8]"Diary of Judge Charles S. Huse," Quoted in Maynard J. Geiger, *Santa Barbara Mission* (Unpublished), Chapter 3, p. 12.

[9]Maynard J. Geiger, O.F.M., "The Apostolic College of Our Lady of Sorrows, Santa Barbara, California (1853-1885)," *Provincial Annals*, XII (July, 1949), 6.

of infecting a great part of society if their progress is not checked.[10]

Amat concluded his ten page pastoral by assuring his people of a "continued prayer on his part for a lasting peace and contentment."

Meanwhile the letters of the Prefect of Propaganda, Alessandro Cardinal Barnabo arrived officially authorizing the property exchange that Amat had requested. But by this time the bishop felt obliged to appeal again to Rome and to the minister general of the Franciscans. Amat's letter to the prefect[11] told of abuses then prevalent among the friars at Santa Barbara, but did not explain their nature. He outlined what he thought should be the dispositions of the friars and concluded with a request for additional Franciscans to accept the post offered by the government at San Luis Rey. In his letter to the minister general, Amat suggested that the establishment at Santa Barbara be abandoned, a plan which he thought would bring an end to the controversy as well as to what were termed "certain scandals" then ravaging the city where "a veritable schism has arisen."[12]

Unfortunately, the situation deteriorated so rapidly that Bishop Amat felt compelled to send one of his close advisors, Father Cajetan Sorrentini, to Rome with a detailed account of all that had happened along with certain proposed remedies. A letter addressed to Pope Pius IX[13] was given to Sorrentini containing, among other things, an outline of the disturbances and their seriousness. At Rome, Sorrentini gave the papers to Cardinal Barnabo, who examined them carefully before submitting them to the Holy

[10]Thaddeus Amat, C.M., *Exhortacion Pastoral* (Santa Barbara, 1856), p. 1.
[11]Dated October 11, 1856.
[12]AALA, *Ristretto*, p. 1.
[13]AALA, Thaddeus Amat to Pius IX, n.p., August 12, 1857.

Father. The accusations were spelled out clearly and the friars were charged with contradicting and discrediting the person of the bishop, of absolving unworthy and unrepentant persons, of neglecting the salvation of souls and of fomenting absurd superstitions among the people. The entire tone of the document, however, was vague. Certainly the friars had not openly and publicly attacked the bishop, although stories to this effect may have reached Amat from people misunderstanding the type of relationship that often exists between the secular and regular clergy. Also it must be pointed out that the friars had no parochial obligations once their transfer had been effected. The mission was a good distance out of town and was not a parish church at this time. Regarding the superstitions, Amat probably had in mind the friars' practice of selling burial shrouds to the faithful, which the latter frequently misinterpreted as being "their key to heaven," and this in spite of the friars' insistence to the contrary.

At Rome the cardinal prefect had informed the Franciscan minister general of the charges and he quickly sent to Santa Barbara for a detailed answer from the friars. In the meantime, the general seems to have taken a decided dislike to Sorrentini,[14] whom h ehad known years earlier in the holy lands, and whom he accused of being anti-Franciscan.[15]

[14]AALA, *Ristretto*, p. 2. This could hardly be denied. Father Cajetan Sorrentini had spent three years in the Holy Lands before joining Bishop Amat in 1854. Born at Rome on August 7, 1815 Sorrentini remained a member of the Roman clergy up to the time of his death at Salinas, June 30, 1893. He once told Pablo de la Guerra that he had been sent to the Holy Lands as a secret "visitor" of the Franciscans by Pius IX. Suspecting their affiliation with the Masons, he reported his findings to Rome. In later years Sorrentini displayed an openly hostile attitude toward anything Franciscan and may very well have been the driving force behind the whole Amat-Franciscan controversy.

[15]A testimonial of Pablo de la Guerra, taken in 1858, notes that "I have never heard from one of them a single word which in any way would becloud or injure

As metropolitan of the ecclesiastical Province of San Francisco, Archbishop Alemany was apprised of the situation by the friars, and as a fellow mendicant his sympathies probably inclined him to aid them in any way he could. His own involvement may have been motivated by his great respect for Father Gonzales Rubio, who had served him as vicar general when Alemany was Bishop of Monterey. In any event, his actions indicated a desire to patch up the situation as quickly as possible.[16] He sent a letter to the minister general[17] which had a marked effect in favor of the Franciscans in Santa Barbara, and the Prefect of Propaganda sent a copy of this letter to Amat at about the same time Sorrentini was presenting his case to the Roman Curia. Previous to the reception of Alemany's letter, Barnabo and the Franciscan general were practically agreed that the Santa Barbara fathers might well give place to others with, as it was expressed, "even greater zeal for the salvation of souls."[18] Alemany's communication, however, caused the whole matter to be restudied at greater length, much to the dismay of Amat, who was anxious for a rapid settlement.

It was the advice of the Archbishop of San Francisco that the minister general appoint a visitor to go to California to study the situation at first hand. This advice was accepted and Father Francisco Caro, a Franciscan then stationed at Saint Joseph's Church, Rossville, Staten Island, New York, was named apostolic visitor.

the high respect due the bishop nor against his person nor against the respect due the secular clergy. . . ."

[16]Alemany is reported to have said, "The illustrious Bishop Amat is well intentioned but according to what you write, it appears that in his manner of thinking he is in error concerning the condition, object and privileges. . . ."

[17]AALA, Joseph S. Alemany to Minister General, n.p., July 3, 1858.

[18]AALA, *Relacion*, n.p., n.d.

Caro arrived by steamer in Santa Barbara on August 26, 1858,[19] and was conducted to the mission where the normal liturgical functions attached to visitations were carried out. The visitor proceeded with his investigation and in the late summer of 1858 made a preliminary report to the minister general which concluded with the observation that "the Franciscans of California enjoy a fine reputation . . . and are worthy of the highest praise."[20]

Bishop Amat was furious with the findings of the Caro report when he read them. He had already become highly incensed at what he considered the unorthodox and imprudent manner of Caro's activities during the visitation. As a matter of fact, there is evidence for believing that the delicate mission had been entrusted to a man of little discretion. Caro had gone first to San Francisco where he had talked at great length with many persons, most of whom knew little or nothing about matters in Santa Barbara and nothing of the priests. Anonymous letters denouncing Bishop Amat were sent to the visitor and were accepted by him as evidence which, needless to say, was contrary to the proper procedure in cases of this nature. In Amat's opinion, the visitor was far from impartial and, in fact, in his judgment Caro seemed to have settled the dispute before ever coming to the actual scene of the disturbance.[21] Even the Franciscan chronicler noted that "the coming of the visitor general stirred up a hornet's nest in California."[22]

Up to this time Amat had been considering, for the sake of peace, allowing the friars to remain at Santa Barbara,

---

[19]Santa Barbara *Gazette,* August 26, 1858.

[20]AALA, Cardinal Barnabo to Thaddeus Amat, certified in *Relacion,* Rome, September 30, 1858.

[21]AALA, Thaddeus Amat to Cardinal Barnabo, n.p., 1858.

[22]Maynard J. Geiger, O.F.M., "The Apostolic College of Our Lady of Sorrows," *Provincial Annals,* XII (October, 1948), 47.

providing that they would promise to adhere strictly to the diocesan regulations which they were not then doing. But any thoughts along these lines were dispelled when he heard that Father Caro had begun collecting signatures on a document attesting to the character of the friars and, it was asserted, even coercing certain individuals to sign against their convictions. Caro's imprudence was further indicated when Amat produced a written assertion by one of Santa Barbara's leading citizens claiming he had been asked "without any explanation"[23] to sign a petition attesting to the honesty of the friars.

At this point the negotiations broke down and the visitor angrily announced to Amat that he had not come to California to hear anything against his own community, which, he claimed, had been unjustly delated to Rome. Amat immediately telegraphed Archbishop Alemany to come to Santa Barbara, repeating his desire to see the matter settled and mentioning the "tumult which is existing among the people and the threat of schism."[24] The archbishop responded at once and upon reaching Santa Barbara inquired of the visitor his reasons for the recent outbreak of antipathy toward the bishop. The evidence that Alemany had assembled, although at first denied, ultimately compelled Caro to admit his predispositions toward the friars. Some time before Father Sorrentini had returned to the diocese and had made his report to the bishop from which Amat concluded that no real solution could be found until he personally went to Rome and presented the matter to Propaganda. He decided upon this course, but before leaving revoked the diocesan faculties from the entire Franciscan community in Santa Barbara,[25]

---

[23]AALA, Daniel Hill statement, Santa Barbara, September 6, 1858.
[24]AALA, *Relacion,* n.p., n.d.
[25]*Ibid.,* September 24, 1858.

an action he took reluctantly, but out of a sincere con-
viction that it was unsafe to allow the friars to continue
their ministry under existing circumstances. His reasons
for this rather drastic action were later given in Rome.[26]
Amat maintained that there were only three friars at Santa
Barbara. Thus they did not constitute a canonical entity
and were, therefore, subject to the ordinary of the diocese
by virtue of a decision of the Sacred Congregation of the
Council on June 4, 1625. He thought their actions warranted this procedure since he had no recourse by civil
law. Repeatedly his verbal admonitions had been ignored
and he feared that open rebellion might arise in his absence if action were not taken.

Soon after his arrival in the Eternal City, the Bishop of
Monterey saw the Cardinal Prefect of Propaganda and
presented his case. While acknowledging his great respect
for the Franciscan pioneers in his diocese, he lamented the
moral decline that had become evident in recent years. The
bishop's grievances embraced the following points:

(1) The friars were admitting youngsters to Holy Commun-
ion without any instructions whatsoever;

(2) All types of public sinners were being given the sacraments, even those known to be burglars, thieves, etc.;

(3) There had been a widespread dissipation of church
goods to those unworthy of such;

(4) The first bishop, Francisco Garcia Diego y Moreno, had
been shamefully treated by the friars during his residence at the mission in Santa Barbara;

(5) Calumnies had been directed toward the bishop and
his curia;

(6) The friars had been unreceptive of all correction on the
part of the bishop;

(7) False indulgences were being granted;

[26]AALA, *Ristretto*, p. 7.

(8) The friars refused to care for needy Indians;
(9) The friars had been begging in the diocese without the proper ecclesiastical permission;
(10) Finally, they had waged a systematic warfare between themselves and the bishop.[27]

Cardinal Barnabo was anxious to have Bishop Amat confer with the Franciscan minister general, the Very Reverend Bernardino de Montefranco, but the latter would agree to a meeting only if, as a previous condition, the friars would be destored their faculties. This, Amat absolutely refused to do for, as he said, "the simple reason that my conscience will not allow it."[28] Finally, however, the prefect was able to bring about a meeting between the two litigants in the course of which Amat said that he and his clergy had been threatened with all types of reprisals as a result of the controversy.[29] He recommended to the cardinal two alternatives, either of which would be perfectly agreeable to him. Namely, "either the Franciscans leave the diocese or he would leave the diocese to the Franciscans."[30]

In defense of the friars, the minister general stated that his priests had always taught the theology of Saint Alphonsus Liguori which he presumed was approved by the Church, and he maintained that the friars not only taught this theology but they lived it. Moreover, he referred to the earlier recommendation of Archbishop Alemany and the testimony of Father Caro as indicative of the worth of his community at Santa Barbara. He also claimed that the testimony of Father Sorrentini was unworthy of considera-

[27]Ibid., p. 6.
[28]AALA, Relacion, n.p., August 17, 1859.
[29]AALA, Ristretto, p. 2.
[30]Ibid.

tion since he was a traditional foe of the order. No specific denials of the other charges are on file, although the minister general in all likelihood had something to say in defense of the remaining accusations. He did claim that Amat's basic intentions for wanting the friars moved from Santa Barbara was his desire to secure the mission for use as his own seminary, unmindful, perhaps, that Amat still held the deed for the mission and had voluntarily turned it over to the Franciscans in the first place.[31]

Bishop Amat placed little value on Alemany's defense of the friars since he alleged that the kindly archbishop had scant knowledge of Santa Barbara, never having spent more than a few days there himself. He pointed out that when the old bishop, Garcia Diego y Moreno, arrived in Santa Barbara to take up his residence in 1841, he had been subjected to innumerable discourtesies and inconveniences.[32] His health was poor and the friars allegedly allowed him to die of hunger in the small quarters of the mission where he was forced to live. This last accusation is certainly not true, but there was evidence that the people of Santa Barbara had little time for their bishop, Franciscan though he was, and that they allowed his hopes and dreams for the diocese to remain "as a monument to the frailty of human speculation."[33]

During the course of the Roman negotiations the Franciscan minister general offered to accept Mission San Luis Rey and to staff it with Italian friars if Amat would allow the ones at Santa Barbara to remain at their post until their reputation had been restored, after which time they

[31]*Ibid.*, pp. 8-9.

[32]This statement was true enough. On one occasion when the bishop's carriage overturned and penned him within, a large crowd of villagers turned and walked away leaving the aged prelate trapped for some hours.

[33]Alfred Robinson, *Life in California* (New York, 1846), p. 239.

would retire to Mexico. But this arrangement, Amat refused to accept.[34] Barnabo then decided to bring the matter directly to the pope and made arrangements for separate audiences for the minister general and Amat. The two sides were presented to Pius IX who promised the litigants that a decision would be handed down as soon a possible. Father Bernardino "strove to vindicate the rights of the College" and later reported that "the whole curia spared itself no labor in this matter."[35] Amat again suggested the action that he thought should be taken, offering several alternatives; one that the Franciscans be transferred to San Luis Rey where 3,000 Catholic Indians were going without the sacraments; another that an impartial apostolic visitor be named; finally, that the Franciscans withdraw completely from his diocese. In addition the bishop made it clear that he had no intentions of leaving Rome until a decision was reached, a fact which he hoped would hasten the final action. And once again he reiterated his willingness "to lay his mitre at the feet of Your Holiness"[36] if such be necessary to restore peace to the diocese.

The decision was rendered on February 13, 1860.[37] It stipulated that the friars were to be given back their diocesan faculties on condition that their superior and his subjects should "humbly and obediently" make such a request to the bishop. In addition, the minister general was told to take immediate action to correct the abuses in question at Santa Barbara. Reports of the corrective measures were to be filed with the proper congregation as soon as possible.

[34]AALA, *Ristretto*, p. 5.

[35]SBMA, III, 160, Bernardino de Montefranco to Gonzales Rubio, Rome, March 20, 1860.

[36]AALA, *Relacion*, n.p., n.d.

[37]AALA, Thaddeus Amat to Joseph S. Alemany, Los Angeles, September 6, 1861.

Almost immediately after the solution of the principal controversy, a second quarrel between the bishop and the friars arose over the interpretation of the word *collegium* and the canonical status of the apostolic college at Santa Barbara. At the outset, the Franciscans had the choice of establishing either a convent or a college. If it was to be a college, then it would be an autonomous institution whose superior had ordinary jurisdiction much like a provincial; whereas, if it was to be a convent, the superior would have only limited powers and would be subject in certain matters to the local bishop. Amat contended that the Santa Barbara foundation was a convent and not a college and was, therefore, subject to his jurisdiction. This contention was denied by the friars who considered their establishment an apostolic college, which, it would seem from the evidence, was actually the case. In 1851, Bishop Alemany of Monterey had petitioned the Holy See on behalf of the Dominicans and Franciscans that "at least one convent or college of each of these Orders be established for the missions of the diocese and that a Novitiate be granted to them." Pius IX had acceded to the request and on February 29, 1852,[38] the official document was issued. Alemany had also asked for approval from the Franciscan minister general and in return, he was given "all the faculties necessary for the purpose of establishing a hospice or college at Mission Santa Barbara or at any other place and authority to receive and invest novices according to the circumstances of the new establishment."[39] The permission, granted by the delegate general, Father Antonio di Rignano, also stipulated that the friars could conduct their own private elections for superiors.

[38]SBMA, II, 1669, Joseph S. Alemany to Pius IX, n.p., February 29, 1852.

[39]SBMA, II, 1673, Delegate-Minister General to Joseph S. Alemany, Rome, April 1, 1852.

As soon as these official documents were received from Rome, the bishop called a meeting at Santa Barbara, which opened on January 5, 1853. There, it was resolved that "this Mission should be turned into a hospice and that the Reverend Father Jose Jimeno, a religious of Saint Francis should be the superior."[40] The document attesting to this agreement was signed by Bishop Joseph Sadoc Alemany; Father Gonzales Rubio, vicar general; Father Jesus Orruno, guardian of the Apostolic College of San Fernando in Mexico City; Father Jose Joaquin Jimeno, prefect of the mission of California and Father Francisco Sanchez, comisario, who had come to California with Bishop Garcia Diego many years earlier. On the following day, Alemany granted his own formal authorization for the establishment which read in part:

> We with the highest gratification of mind concede to them that they may establish an hospice and college for the missions of their Order at Mission Santa Barbara, or, if this be deemed unsuitable, in any other place designated in Our Diocese, so that missionaries may go forth to convert to our Faith the pagan natives . . .[41]

Three months later, Alemany handed over to the Franciscans the mission at Santa Barbara for the purpose of opening an apostolic college "in such a way, however, that the Very Rev. Fr. Gonzales Rubio remain pastor of the congregation as long as he may desire . . ."[42] Unfortunately, the old mission buildings proved utterly unsuitable for the friars and they were forced to ask Alemany's permission to purchase a more promising site, preferably within the city.

---

[40]Zephryin Engelhardt, O.F.M., *Missions and Missionaries of California* (San Francisco, 1912), IV, 703.

[41]SBMA, III, 1, Joseph S. Alemany to Franciscans, Santa Barbara, January 6, 1853.

[42]SBMA, III, 8, Joseph S. Alemany to Joaquin Jimeno, San Francisco, April 18, 1853.

The bishop agreed and thus a location was found and a college inaugurated on July 23, 1854, at State and Figueroa Streets in downtown Santa Barbara. It was Alemany's wish that the friars make the college facilities available to the townspeople in order to serve the double purpose of being close to the spiritual needs of the people and of securing from them a revenue sufficient for their maintenance.[43]

With the transfer of Alemany to San Francisco in 1853, the college lost its principal benefactor, for the new bishop was noticeably unsympathetic toward it from the very beginning. Amat's attitude may have been motivated by the thought that the Franciscans were seeking immunity from his jurisdiction, a privilege which earlier apostolic colleges in Mexico and South America had enjoyed by virtue of their charters. As matters turned out, Amat was known to have written Alemany on one occasion offering the opinion that the friars were acting "above and beyond" the laws of the diocese in a manner he could not tolerate.[44] It is not immediately clear how Amat felt he could press this claim, because the friars went to great lengths to convince him that they had a canonically erected college at Santa Barbara. Amat was shown all the documents in the mission archives attesting to the foundation's juridical status. But he remained unimpressed and merely replied, "the evidence is lacking!" As a matter of fact, it was generally accepted in Rome, Zacatecas and Mexico City that the intention of the founders was to erect a genuine and fully outfitted apostolic college with all the privileges and immunities enjoyed thereby.

In the meantime, Archbishop Alemany let it be known in late August of 1861 that he had received an apostolic

[43]SBMA, III, 40, Statement of Gonzales Rubio, Santa Barbara, July 23, 1854.

[44]AALA, Thaddeus Amat to Joseph S. Alemany, n.p., September 8, 1861.

brief delegating him to arbitrate the contentions between the friars and the bishop which he hoped could be done on an impartial basis. "The delicate difficulty," as he put it, "has fallen into my humble hands."[45] In retrospect, it would seem that Rome made a poor selection in Alemany since it was he who had been instrumental in bringing about the foundation of the college in the first place, and he could scarcely be expected, therefore, to be objective. His respect for Father Rubio and to the "other founders of our diocese" was a widely known fact. In a letter to Bishop Amat, Alemany outlined his approach to the problem, although at this time he seems to have lacked certain of the necessary documents. He said,

> Now my good brother, at those early days I lived nowhere and everywhere, and it was very difficult to keep all records very accurate. Can anyone suppose . . . that I would not grant them what they wanted? and this was my meaning in entering the record.[46]

In other words, Alemany acknowledged that it had been his intention to allow the friars to begin an apostolic college when the original request was made.

Soon after a visit paid to Santa Barbara in January, 1862, the archbishop told Amat, "I must confess that my opinion of the goodness of the Fathers of Santa Barbara, and of their good regard for you, was much strengthened at my last visit to that place."[47] He urged Amat to re-examine carefully the generally good reputation of the fathers, what they had suffered and what they deserved as the founders

[45]AALA, Joseph S. Alemany to Thaddeus Amat, San Francisco, August 27, 1861.

[46]AALA, Joseph S. Alemany to Thaddeus Amat, San Francisco, September 22, 1861.

[47]AALA, Joseph S. Alemany to Thaddeus Amat, San Francisco, February 18, 1862.

of the diocese. He ended his letter with the plea that peace would soon come about. Bishop Amat, however, felt it necessary to ignore the disputed prerogatives of the college until definitive word arrived from the Holy See. He was unable, therefore, to ordain any Franciscan students, maintaining as he did that their dimissorial letters were invalid, since the superior of the college did not have ordinary jurisdiction.

In an effort to arrive at a clearer understanding of the dispute, Archbishop Alemany sent Amat a copy of the original permission he had given to the friars to erect a college along with the following observation:

> I know it was always a question of a missionary college and for that reason I urged the guardian of San Fernando to come up with me all the way from Mexico. I had no other intention than to carry on their views.[48]

Amat's response was surprising, considering that he had apparently seen identical documentation from the mission archives. He wrote:

> I feel thankful to you for such a document, had I got it two years ago! I had always learned from the writings of the Franciscan Fathers themselves that the nature of an Apostolic College is that it cannot be transferred but by the authority of the Holy See and you granted them said faculty with the condition that 'hac inutili considerata, in alio loco designando in hac Diocesi,' may be transferred and still all the difficulty that has existed between me and them came from having transferred them . . . although this was done by the authority of the Holy See.[49]

The bishop went on to point out that the friars would seem to have been given the authority to establish the house in the *mission,* but *not in the town* where they actually did

[48]AALA, Joseph S. Alemany to Thaddeus Amat, San Francisco, April 10, 1862.
[49]AALA, Thaddeus Amat to Joseph S. Alemany, Los Angeles,April 22, 1862.

found the college. The greatest insight of the whole en-
tangled dispute, perhaps, was Amat's opinion that,

> They intended to have their house independent even from
> their Minister General, who avowed that he never had any
> communication from the RR Franciscans from California or
> Mexico until I had recourse to them.[50]

Both of these statements were obviously unfounded, for
it is doubtful that the Franciscans ever tried to establish
themselves as an independent authority; in fact, a procedure of this type would never have been tolerated. Nor
did the friars act without the knowledge of their general,
as was evidenced by earlier documentation.

The controversy dragged on for years. But due to the
kindly moderation of the metropolitan there were no further violent outbreaks on either side. In the winter of 1876
and 1877 there was some correspondence between Alemany and Amat relative to the question; the archbishop
suggested, as he had done on many previous occasions,
that the parish in the town of Santa Barbara be returned to
the friars. It was Alemany's contention that the Franciscan
college at Santa Barbara was financially ruining the friars.
Actually, Amat had advanced a large sum of money to the
Franciscans in January, 1876, but notwithstanding, the
archbishop also thought that "when Padre Antonio Jimeno
agreed to retain the mission and give up the parish church
of Our Lady of Sorrows, he likely exceeded his powers."
The archbishop felt that the friars could support themselves if they were given back the parish and allowed to
solicit alms.

The Franciscan-Amat controversies certainly do not form
one of the brighter chapters in the history of the Catholic
Church in California. They seemed to owe their origin to

[50]*Ibid.*

a genuine misunderstanding on the part of Bishop Amat which the passage of time seemed only to increase.[51] Individual actions were misinterpreted and exaggerated out of perspective by both parties, and it would be unfair to place the blame wholly on either side for these unhappy events. In fairness to Amat, however, it must be said that the existing documents on these cases sustain his contentions, especially in regard to the earlier charges made by the bishop, for no evidence has been discovered that the friars attempted any more than a blanket denial of the accusations.[52] As an epilogue to the disputes, it is pleasant to add that rancor and personal feeling would seem to have speedily disappeared on both sides. In fact, there is abundant evidence that Amat had kindly personal feelings toward the friars and they toward him. He went out of his way on several occasions to make his views as clear and concise as possible "so that you will understand that my action is not the result of any lack of esteem for your Community . . . but rather a sense of principle and duty."[53] Some years later when they were beset with financial difficulties the bishop borrowed $17,000 from the Hibernian Bank in his own name and used the reputation of his office to help

[51]That there were those whose selfish interests were furthered by the unpleasant controversy is hardly deniable and the respected Pablo de la Guerra ventured the opinion that "here we are confronted with a plan concocted and pursued by some who have attempted to dispose the bishop unfavorably to the Reverend Franciscan Fathers." SBMA, III, 112, Testimonial, Santa Barbara, 1858.

[52]An eleven page letter written to the Franciscan Minister General in 1883 by a member of the community at Santa Barbara outlines in great detail the poor state of discipline at the mission. In referring to this letter some years ago, the eminent Franciscan historian, Maynard J. Geiger, observed that it was "both comic and tragic. Comic because of the strange, rare style, and ungrammatical sentences of the man who wrote it; tragic because of the fact that there was at least a basis for some of the things he stated. . . ." Cf. SBMA, III, 663, Bonaventure Fox to Minister General, Santa Barbara, December 17, 1883.

[53]SBMA, III, Thaddeus Amat to Jose Romo, Los Angeles, April 22, 1873.

the community through a difficult time.[54] And the year before his death Amat's name was enrolled in the Franciscan Mass book by Father Joseph Romo who referred to him "as the worthy bishop of Monterey-Los Angeles."[55]

[54]SBMA, III, 534, Promissory note of Jose Romo to Thaddeus Amat, Santa Barbara, January 1, 1878.

[55]Even those who disagreed with the bishop characterized him as "a just man, hard-working and active, and a bishop zealous in the fulfillment of his episcopal duties." Cf. SBMA, III, 1112, Testimonial, Santa Barbara, 1858.

CHAPTER FOUR

THE PIOUS FUND OF THE CALIFORNIAS

Soon after the hostilities between the United States and Mexico had been concluded, the United States Congress passed legislation establishing a Commission to settle private land titles in the State of California previously granted by Mexico. Those claims judged valid were recognized as such by the American Government. It was in accordance with this legislation that Bishop Joseph Sadoc Alemany presented his request that all Church property then in possession of religious persons or institutions be legally confirmed.

It was also in 1851 that the California State Legislature appointed a Committee to investigate the subject of the Pious Fund. Their final report, inconclusive as it was, related only that there had been such a Fund at one time consisting of large amounts of securities.

At the first Synod held in the Diocese of Monterey, which commenced on March 19, 1852,[1] the priests in attendance urged Bishop Alemany to examine the possibility of making a settlement with the Mexican Government on the Pious Fund. The next year, the Bishop at-

---

[1] AALA, "Libro Borrador," p. 275 (entry for March 10).

tended the First Plenary Council of Baltimore where he received similiar advice:

> I conferred with the Archbishop of Baltimore and other prelates on the large debt due from Mexico to our Church and mission in California.[2]

The Bishop also discussed the matter with Chief Justice Roger Taney who suggested that he present his claim "before the United States Land Commission in California empowered by Congress to determine all kinds of land claims in the State."

At the express request of the American hierarchy, Bishop Alemany then personally journeyed to Mexico City where he vainly attempted to obtain redress from the openly hostile Government:

> I demanded that satisfaction be made to our Church in California, that as successor to Bishop Garcia Diego, I justly demanded for my missions and for my diocese; and that they should cease also to oppose my administration in Lower California.[3]

The determination of the Dominican Bishop is obvious from his entries in the Libro Borrador:

> During July and August I continued to demand of the Mexican Government that above, and after many delays they notified me they could not accede to my demands and so I left the capital.[4]

No further action was taken by the Bishop until late in 1855 when he turned over all his available documentation to his attorney, John Thomas Doyle, who was to figure prominently in the complicated legislation for the next forty-five years.

---

[2]*Ibid.*, p. 275 (entry for May 18); Peter Guilday, *History of the Councils of Baltimore*, (New York, 1932), p. 177.

[3]*Ibid.*, p. 275 (entry for July).

[4]*Ibid.*, p. 276 (entry for 1852).

The existence of such a Fund in that country was known to all the old inhabitants of the State, although none appeared to have any definite information about it, and even a legislative investigation in 1851 had failed to bring anything to light about it. I saw no probable way to obtain anything from Mexico for it until another claims commission should be made with the country and advised the Archbishop to wait in hope of such.[5]

In the meantime, a Metropolitan Province had been erected with its seat at San Francisco, and the Archbishop of San Francisco continued to act on behalf of Bishop Amat in the litigation pertaining to the Pious Fund.

The Archbishop took no action until the spring of 1857, at which time he again called on Mr. Doyle and proposed to engage his services, along with those of Mr. Eugene Casserly in an effort to bring about a settlement of the case.

Mr. Doyle proceeded to draw up an *informe*. The earlier correspondence between General Valencia, one-time Administrator of the Fund and Don Pedro Ramirez, lawyer of the Right Reverend Francisco Garcia Diego y Moreno, O.F.M., first Bishop of Both Californias, which the Archbishop found among the papers of his predecessor, provided much of the source material needed for later briefs.

> And here Don Pedro Ramirez's methodical discharge of duty proved of incalculable value to me. His *"Instruccion Circumstancia,"* named each piece of property, urban and rural, which he delivered over. . . . These names enabled me to identify the property and trace its acquisition . . . in the succeeding eleven years, I picked up the material of the history.[6]

The political ferment in Mexico in those days made formal submission of the case a practical impossibility.

---

[5] John T. Doyle, *The Case of the Pious Fund of California in the International Arbitral Court* (San Francisco, 1906), p. 3.

[6] Sister Mary Imelda Quinn, "The Case of the Pious Fund of California in the International Court of the Hague, 1902" (unpupublished thesis, Loyola University, Los Angeles, 1935), p. 30.

However, Doyle did file a letter with the Secretary of State on July 20, 1859, alerting the American Government of the Church's claim.[7]

Meanwhile in 1868, Doyle's business associate, Eugene Casserly was elected to the United States Senate representing California, an event which subsequently proved of great assistance to the litigation. On July 4th, at a Convention between the United States and Mexico, the long-awaited American and Mexican Mixed Commission was set up to settle claims of citizens of either country against the other that had arisen during the interval of February 3rd, 1848 and February 1st, 1869.

> Down to that time (Casserly's election to the Senate) I had, after every session of Congress, examined the laws and treaties to see if any convention for claims had been concluded with Mexico, but after the election of my associate to the Senate, I naturally relied on him for such information; but he seems to have forgotten in the multipilicity of political business all about the Pious Fund, and I was ignorant of the convention of 1868 until the 27th of March, 1870, when I casually saw mentioned in a New York paper that Wednesday, the 31st of that month, would be the last day for presenting claims to the American and Mexican Mixed Commission, sitting in Washington.[8]

Mr. Doyle acted quickly as we see from his own narrative:

> The Pious Fund as a case in my charge had so long appeared a hopeless one. . . . I soon got hold of the Convention of July 4th, 1868. . . . Demands made under it were limited to injuries to persons or property committed by either Republic on the citizens of the other, since the date of the Treaty of Guadalupe-Hidalgo, February 2, 1848. It was soon clear that the wrong done in seizing the Pious Fund and taking it into the

[7] John T. Doyle, *Memorial of the Claims of the California Bishops* (San Francisco, 1871), p. 11.

[8] John T. Doyle, *The Case of the Pious Fund of California in the International Arbitral Court*, p. 5.

public Treasury in 1842 could not be made a subject of recla-
mation under the Convention. . . . I determined to waive all
claims for the property of the Fund, and to treat Santa Ana's
decree as a *bona fide* purchase of it . . . and demand damages
for the nonpayment of the installments of the interest accrued
by the treaty of Guadalupe-Hidalgo.[9]

Archbishop Alemany and Bishop Amat were both in
Rome attending the Vatican Council, a fact which necessitated Doyle's using the *epikeia* clause which allowed him
to proceed with the case, but on his own authority.

Mr. Doyle immediately sent Senator Casserly a telegram
authorizing him to act for the archbishop:

Present to Joint Commission sitting in Washington a claim by
Archbishop Alemany and Bishop Amat, successors of Francisco
Garcia Diego, Bishop of Californias, on behalf of themselves
and all interested, for the income of proceeds of property belonging to Pious Fund of the Missions of California. . . . This
claim first became due American citizens by treaty of Quere-
taro, whereby both trustees and beneficiaries became American. . . . All rents and proceeds received since February 2,
1848 fall within Convention of July 4th, 1868; prior spoliations
released. Thursday is last day.[10]

Senator Casserly, in accordance with the directives made
in this message, submitted the claim to the Mixed Commission in time to obtain a hearing. Since Doyle had acted
upon his own initiative, and not according to the terms of
his earlier agreement with the bishops, he had considered
it necessary to have his telegram countersigned by the Very
Reverend James Croke, Vicar General of the San Francisco Archdiocese. As a matter of fact, Doyle wrote later
that "the clients were entirely satisfied with my proceed-

[9]Quoted in Sister Mary Imelda Quinn, *cp. cit.,* p. 31.

[10]John T. Doyle, *The Case of the Pious Fund of California in the International
Arbitral Court,* p. 6.

ings and Archbishop Alemany expressed cordially his gratification at it."[11]

Doyle gathered the evidence together for presentation to the Commission by Nathaniel Wilson and Philip Phillips who were acting for Senator Casserly. Father Hugh Gallagher, who was in Washington and who had power of attorney for the California bishops, verified the Memorial and it was subsequently filed before the Commission.

The Memorial was heavily documented with statistical information relevant to the Church in the Californias. It emphasized that after the purchase of Upper California in 1848, Mexico had failed to make a single payment from the accumulated interest of the Pious Fund as pledged by Santa Ana in 1842.[12]

Mexico was defended by the brilliant lawyer, Caleb Cushing who asked immediately for dismissal of the charges, a move analogus to that made in a common court of law to non-suit a plantiff on the opening of his counsel. This legal maneuver was justified on the following grounds:

(1) The act of incorporation of petitioners as corporators sole did not authorize them to claim property beyond the limit of the State of California;

(2) The petitioners showed no legal title in or to the Pious Fund;

(3) The petitioners had a legal remedy in the courts of Mexico, which they were bound to pursue and exhaust before coming here;

(4) The injuries complained of in this case were done before the treaty of Guadalupe-Hidalgo, 1848. The Commission, therefore, had no jurisdiction with the claim.[13]

[11]*Ibid.*, p. 6.

[12]The *Memorial* is included in a series of fourteen pamphlets printed between 1871 and 1880 and issued under the title, *Some Accounts of the Pious Fund of California* (San Francisco). This valuable book contains briefs, arguments, memorials and other papers relating to the history of the case.

Cushing wanted the case dismissed immediately but this motion was denied by the Court. Actually, "Mr. Cushing's motion to dismiss was never formally passed to my knowledge," according to Doyle.

The claim of the bishops of California pointed out that there had accrued to the Roman Catholics of California on October 24th, 1848, and on that day every succeeding year to February 1st, 1869, an obligation on the part of the Mexican Government to pay an annual interest on the Pious Fund. The American case concluded with the following observation:

> Certainly a more equitable claim could not be presented for consideration. A fund contributed by Catholics, in various countries, for converting to the Catholic faith the Indians of California, is taken possession of by the Mexican government and used for its own purposes, on the understanding that it would make an annual payment as a substitute thereof. The work to which this fund was dedicated by the donors remains uncompleted; there are Indians in California not yet gathered into the bosom of the Church. The proper representatives of that Church now call upon the Mexican Government for those annual payments, that they may carry out the benevolent purpose of those who contributed of their private property the means for its accomplishment; and we may say, using the mildest terms, that it does not become the integrity or dignity of Mexico, that she should seek, through legal subtleties, to avoid the fulfillment of an obligation incurred under such circumstances.[14]

Additional evidence was offered between March 1st, 1873 and the following October 30th. The case was placed before the Commission for a decision on May 19th, 1875. The American Commissioner, William Wadsworth, filed

[13]Cf. *Brief of P. Phillips and N. Wilson in Reply to the Motion to Dismiss the Petition* (San Francisco, 1871) for the full text of the dismissal motion.

[14]*Ibid.*, a quotation of the umpire in the case of Isaac Moses, the 24th of April, 1871, with the conclusion added by Phillips and Wilson.

claims for $904,700.79 while his Mexican counterpart, De Zamacona, strenuously denied that any funds were due the claim. The Mixed Commission, having reached a deadlock, submitted the case to an umpire, Sir Edward Thornton, British Ambassador to the United States.

Both parties submitted new evidence to the Arbitrator who handed down his decision on November 11, 1875, in favor of the claimants. He fixed the value of the Pious Fund at $1,433,033 at the time of its sale in 1842. He awarded the amount of $904,700.79[15] (amended October 24th, 1876 to $904,070.79) [16] in Mexican gold, which was twenty-one years interest at the rate of $43,080.99 per annum, of 6% of one half the capitalized value of the Pious Fund. Sir Edward decreed an equal amount to the ecclesiastical officials in Baja California.

> After a careful examination of the data furnished, with regard to the yearly amount of the interest, the Umpire is constrained to adopt the views of the Commissioner of the United States.
>
> There is no doubt that the Mexican Government must have in its possession all the documents and all the accounts relative to the sale of the property belonging to the Pious Fund and the proceeds thereof; yet these have not been produced, and the only inference that can be drawn from silence upon this subject is that the amounts of the proceeds, actually received into the Treasury, was at least not less than it is claimed to be.[17]

The subject of *res judicata*, on which the Mexican Government based its case, was not allowed by the Commission for several reasons, some of which can be summarized thusly:

[15] An equal amount went to Baja California, for in the words of the umpire, "there can be little doubt that Lower California needs the beneficial assistance of the Pious Fund as much as, and even more. . . ."

[16] The amendment was necessary due to a mathematical error in the figures submitted by the accountants to Sir Edward Thornton.

[17] Sir Edward Thornton, *Decision of the Umpire* (San Francisco, 1871), p. 6.

(1) The Mixed Commission did not have the right to make a judgment on this case which it proceeded to do;

(2) The Mixed Commission was entitled to interpret the Convention of 1868 and its rulings;

(3) Mexico waived any right to object to the jurisdiction of the Mixed Commission by entering upon the trial without reservations;

(4) The principal of *res judicata* applies to arbitral decisions and to the findings of international commissions.

In accordance with the decision handed down by Sir Edward Thornton, Mexico made the first installment payment on January 31st, 1877.

DISTRIBUTION OF THE FUNDS

At the request of Archbishop Alemany, Bishop Amat informed the Holy See about the Pious Fund litigation early in 1859. He explained in a letter to Cardinal Barnabo the needs of the Church in California and the legalities then contemplated for recovery of the Fund from Mexico. Bishop Amat asked the Prefect of the Congregation of Propaganda Fide to tell the Holy Father of the action and secure his approval.[18]

There is no available evidence that the pope encouraged the bishops to proceed with their claims. At that particular time, the relations between the Holy See and Mexico were rapidly deteriorating and a statement from Pope Pius would only have infuriated an already hostile Government.

Archbishop Alemany, as early as December 19th, 1875, thought it wise to ask the Holy See for a directive which would facilitate an equitable distribution of the Pious Fund, if and when a favorable verdict was rendered:

---

[18]AALA, "Diocese of Monterey and Los Angeles, Roman Documents, Decrees and Faculties, 1896," p. 36, entry No. 45, Thaddeus Amat to Cardinal Barnabo, Los Angeles, n.d.

I think it proper to ask the Holy See for some kind of general faculty to use what we may receive, first and principally for the Indians, their Christian education and any aid required for them; then a good portion might be devoted to our schools, asylums and colleges according to their need, and some might be given to the churches, particularly those that most need it. And I would suggest that each Bishop act then with some advice of his consulters and keep an account, so that hereafter no one may blame us, as if we had abused the Fund.[19]

Shortly after the decision had been handed down, the Archbishop wrote again to Bishop Amat regarding the apportionment of monies:

Every Bishop naturally loves his Diocese, sees the wants and desires to make provision to meet them, and no doubt each of us might wish to have a large share to meet his necessities. But as the Fund was not only for the conversions of the Indians, but also for that of the pagans and also for the maintainance of Christians in the Californias and as if it should be difficult to estimate the various wants of each Diocese, to carry out those objectives, and as Utah Territory with the exception of a small portion of the south part of the Colorado river, formed part of the Californias, and yet is not part of my Diocese, I would therefore propose that whatever be received after giving a large donation to the Franciscan and Jesuit Fathers, be equally divided between the four places, viz., the three Dioceses of this Province and the Territory of Utah . . .[20]

The proposals ultimately drawn up by the archbishop and his two suffragans were submitted to Rome for consideration. On March 7th, 1877, His Eminence, Alexander Cardinal Franchi presented the decision of his consultors for approval by Pope Pius IX. The proposals can be summarized briefly.

[19]AALA, Joseph S. Alemany to Thaddeus Amat, San Francisco, December 19, 1876.

[20]AALA, Joseph S. Alemany to Thaddeus Amat, San Francisco, December 20, 1876.

$26,000 was to be paid to the heirs of Jose Antonio Aguirre, in payment for a loan made in 1842; $24,000 was to go to the Archbishop of Oregon City (now Portland) for missions in his province, (especially the Vicariate of Idaho); $40,000 was to be divided equally between the Fathers of the Order of Saint Francis and those of the Society of Jesus; and of the remainder, seven equal parts were to be made, of which one was to be assigned in perpetuity to the missions of Utah; and the other six were to be divided equally among the three bishops of the Province of San Francisco.[21]

[21] AALA, "Diocese (*ut supra*) . . .," p. 93, March 4, 1877.

CHAPTER FIVE

DIOCESAN EXPANSION

IT WAS late in 1855 that the decision relating to California
Catholic property interests was made by the United States
Land Commission. By this decision the Church had restored to it the titles of missions, cemeteries and certain adjacent lands and gardens.[1] In its verdict the court ruled
that the Mexican governors and their mission administra-
tors lacked the authority to dispose of church buildings,
the priest's residence and the few surrounding acres. Although the favorable verdict was not unexpected, nevertheless, it gave new hope for restoration of divine worship
and immediate establishment of regular parish life in the
larger centers of population. Of the twenty-five missions,
sixteen, stretching from San Diego in the south to Santa
Cruz and San Juan Bautista in the north, were in the Diocese of Monterey. Amat was thus the principal beneficiary
of a decision that owed its success to the labors of Archbishop Alemany who had been pressing the claims since
his arrival in California.[2]

[1]An entry in the *Libro Borrador* for December 28 mentions that the United
States District Attorney appealed the decision. A later note on November 26, 1856
states that the appeal was dismissed by the United States Government.

[2]Specifically mentioned in the verdict were Missions San Diego, San Luis Rey,
San Juan Capistrano, San Gabriel, San Buenaventura and Santa Barbara. Cf. The
Chronicle, December 22, 1855, for a complete transcript of the decision.

The judgment of the commission was rendered "without prejudice" to the interests of third parties, that is to say, it was a decision of right as between the bishops of California on the one hand and on the other of those who held the properties by grant, sale or lease after the missions had been secularized, and that particularly in the years immediately preceding American occupation in California. For more than two decades the occasional claims to these properties had caused a great deal of litigation which, with few exceptions, had an issue favorable to the bishops. Unfortunately, the defense of the Church's titles was a heavy burden at a time when the revenue of the diocese was urgently needed for other types of apostolic work. The decision of the commission served to recapitulate the principles laid down in all the law books regarding the right to property by dedication. Former legal status was re-emphasized, namely, that while the naked title was in the government, the usufruct constituted a right to the estate which would never have been violated in justice. Church property in Mexican times was known as a class of property standing by itself in legal nomenclature and governed by laws not applicable to other estates. Its intention was to protect and perpetuate its use to the benefit of the Church.[3]

Most of the restored missions were badly damaged by years of neglect and a few were in ruins. Their restoration to ecclesiastical title was timely, however, not only for their usefulness in present needs, but as evidence of the spirit of justice which moved the United States Government to act favorably in this matter. In the late 1850's and early 1860's Presidents Buchanan and Lincoln were to sign

[3]Jackson H. Ralston, *Foreign Relations of the United States, Appendix II, 1902* (Washington, 1903), 420. A thorough discussion is contained in Jackson's work on the legal aspects of the case.

several patents which completed the formal process of recognition of the proprietary rights of the Catholic Church to these historic landmarks.

PHYSICAL ADDITIONS

There were only sixteen churches in the Diocese of Monterey in 1854 when Thaddeus Amat came to California, and five of these were ruined missions. By the time of his death a quarter century later, the indefatigable Vincentian had raised that number to include thirty churches, eight public chapels, an equal number of oratories and twenty-six mission stations, most of which were at least frame buildings.

First of the churches authorized by Amat was that of San Salvador in the Jurupa Mountain range near present-day Riverside. In its earliest days the little church was cared for by the priests at San Gabriel. Late in 1857 plans were made for a church at Montecito near Santa Barbara. Sixteen acres were acquired from Dona Alaya in 1857 and on March 1st[4] the bishop personally presided at corner-stone laying ceremonies bestowing the title of Our Lady of Mount Carmel on the new edifice.

The old mission church at Santa Cruz suffered considerable damage by earthquakes in 1840 and 1857 and in February of that latter year the southwest corner of the building was so weakened by the winter rains that it was no longer safe for public use. Despite the fact that 1857 found the Diocese of Monterey in a precarious financial condition, Bishop Amat made plans for a new church in the area and went there on July 5th[5] for the initial cere-

[4]Zephryin Engelhardt, O.F.M., *Santa Barbara Mission* (San Francisco, 1923), p. 403.

[5]AALA, *"Libro Gobierno,"* p. 32.

monies. Designed for a capacity of 350 persons, the building was erected by Walters and Beck of Santa Cruz. So diligently did the construction company and Father Benito Capdevila work that the completed edifice was ready for dedication on July 14, 1858. The bishop was present for the occasion and gave the church an Anglo-sized version of its former title, the Exaltation of the Holy Cross.

The City of Anaheim was established in 1857 by a group of German settlers although there were likely few if any Catholics in the immediate area for some years after. In 1858, however, Don Bernardo Yorba "ordered the erection of a church in the locality now known as Yorba." Shortly before his death later in the year, Yorba deeded the partially completed adobe church to the Diocese of Monterey-Los Angeles. Bishop Thaddeus Amat conferred the title of San Antonio de Padua on the new foundation which was blessed on April 29, 1860 by Father Blasius Raho, C.M., the Vicar General. In subsequent years the church became a mission to Saint Boniface and in 1875 received its first pastor in the person of the Reverend Victor Fauron.[6]

Parochial beginnings in Visalia also date from 1860 when a temporary structure was put up under the patronage of the Nativity of the Blessed Virgin, a title later shortened to Saint Mary's. As the governmental seat of Tulare County, Visalia had long needed its own church facilities. Saint Joseph's Chapel at nearby Havilah City was erected in 1862 to succeed the crumbling mission station of San Emigdio. Known throughout the state as one of the leading areas for high grade ore, the city was heavily populated in the 1860's but after 1879 most of its people moved down from the hill regions into the valley.

---

[6]Donald Montrose, *The Making of a Parish* (Anaheim, 1961), p. 35.

Catholics in San Bernardino had been clamoring for a church for some years. Now almost deserted by its early Mormon settlers, the recent development of mining in and around the city, particularly in Holcombe Valley, had brought new colonizers to the area. Bishop Amat and his close advisor, Judge Benjamin Hayes, visited the desert city and were impressed by the apparent need for ecclesiastical facilities. The little church at Agua Mensa erected in 1853, overlooking the Santa Ana River, had been destroyed by flood as had the even smaller chapel at Jurupa. The townspeople were anxious to build a central church at San Bernardino which would serve the needs of the whole area. Later that summer, on July 7th, Father Raho journeyed out to inspect the site and celebrated Holy Mass for the Catholic inhabitants. Hayes recorded the trip in his diary:

I must long remember the wearisome canon from Holcombe Valley to the mouth, from the visit I made with Rev. Father Raho shortly before his death, to Holcombe. It was then full of miners, but they were poor. Their pious contributions aided one of his dearest objects, the repair of the church at Los Angeles, which had been injured by the rains of January. There is a marked significance in the gilt inscription placed on its front.[7]

A temporary church was in operation by 1863 and plans made for the establishment of additional stations at San Jacinto and Temascal. Tragedy struck on the night of October 2, 1866 when fire, possibly of an incendiary nature, destroyed the Church. The act caused such general indignation that on October 6th, a mass meeting was held in the courthouse presided over by Judge Shulett Clark.[8] Father Peter Verdaguer, the pastor, described the extent of the damage and a committee of three was named to urge a

[7]Benjamin J. Hayes, *Pioneer Notes* (Los Angeles, 1929), p. 278.
[8]APF, Thaddeus Amat to Propagation de la Foi, Washington, February 8, 1867.

suitable reward for the apprehension of the culprit, and another committee of seven members headed a campaign for the rebuilding. When the bishop was informed of the action taken, he was most grateful to the generous people of San Bernardino and heartily endorsed their action. By 1870 funds had been collected by Father Thomas Donohue for a large new building and on July 9, 1871 Bishop Amat dedicated the Church of Saint Bernardine of Sienna. Choniclers noted that he

> confirmed thirty-five in the church at Agua Mensa. That evening solemn vespers and benediction was presided over by the Bishop . . .[9]

The first records of a Catholic Church in Gilroy date from November 12, 1854 when Archbishop Alemany dedicated a chapel to Saint Martin. With the arrival of Father Thomas Hudson in 1864 plans were made for a new building and through the hearty support and cooperation of his parishioners Saint Mary's Church was ready for use in 1866.[10]

A modest little church was dedicated at modern Wilmington on November 29, 1865 under the patronage of Saint Peter.[11] The next year saw plans materialize for a church of Saint Vincent de Paul in Los Angeles. A cornerstone was set in place in July of 1866 but the unfinished building was gutted by fire soon thereafter.[12]

The Church of Our Lady of Sorrows at Santa Barbara, which had been dedicated on July 29, 1855, as successor

> After the Gospel, the Bishop delivered an eloquent discourse on the dedication ceremony and when mass ended, he administered confirmation to ten children. The day previous, he had

[9]Condensed from the San Bernardino *Guardian,* June 28, 1871.
[10]Gilroy *Gazette,* June 14, 1907.
[11]AALA, *"Libro Gobierno,"* p. 52.
[12]Present-day Saint Vincent's Parish dates only from 1887.

to the old presidio chapel, also succumbed to fire in August of 1865. Fortunately the glass and metal case housing the relics of Saint Vibiana escaped unharmed. The adjoining presbytery was saved but the extensive damage amounted to over $6,000 and only through the kindness of Archbishop Alemany was it possible to raise funds for rebuilding the church. Alemany commented editorially that "the people of Santa Barbara have suffered terribly by last year's drought," a fact which "justifies them in appealing to our liberality."[13] Appealing to Propagation de la Foi in Paris, Amat told the director that with all its troubles "surely the Council has no poorer diocese with which to deal."[14]

When the centennial of the first mission in the state was held in San Diego on July 18, 1869 Bishop Amat preached both in English and Spanish at a Mass celebrated by the Reverend Maurice O'Brien, C.M., of Saint Vincent's College. Immediately after Vespers the bishop laid the cornerstone of the new Saint Joseph's Church.[15] Three years later, on April 20, 1872, Old Town was destroyed by fire and the pastor, Father Anthony Ubach decided to relocate the church on a mesa west of town. A frame edifice was dedicated by Coadjutor Bishop Francis Mora on January 31, 1875.

On August 30, 1872 Amat offered the friars at Santa Barbara the orphan asylum and church in the Pajaro Valley near Watsonville. The original foundation there had been made in 1854 and was known as Our Lady Help of Christians but from 1857 onwards it went under the title of Im-

---

[13]San Francisco *Bulletin,* August 30, 1865.

[14]AALA, Thaddeus Amat to Propagation de la Foi, Los Angeles, October 24, 1865.

[15]A little chapel was erected at "Slabtown" (later Cambria Pines) in 1869. It was named Santa Rosa.

maculate Heart. The friars formally accepted charge of
the parish and Saint Francis Orphanage for Boys[16] on January 7, 1874. The following year, a chapel to Our Lady of
Mount Carmel was put into operation at Aptos, near Santa
Cruz.[17]

Although its history goes back as far as 1861, parochial
beginnings at Watsonville date only from May 9, 1875. On
that date Bishop Mora "dedicated the parochial church of
this town . . . under the invocation of Saint Patrick."

Property was acquired for a church at Castroville in November of 1865 and a cemetery in 1873. Originally cared
for by priests from Monterey, it was only in 1869 that
Father Hugh Curran went to Castroville as the first resident pastor. He built a small chapel which, in later years,
became the sacristy of the large church. Ceremonies were
held on October 3, 1875 in the largely Irish agricultural
community to formally inaugurate the recently completed
edifice.

Yet with all the emphasis on material construction, Amat
never allowed these things to interfere with the spiritual
life of his people as was evident from the following newspaper account of the annual Corpus Christi procession for
1865:

> The old-time practice in Southern California settlements of
> keeping up the Feast of Corpus Christi was observed with the
> usual ceremonies and by crowds of natives and other Catholics
> in all the old Mission parishes on Tuesday, June 15th. This is
> the time of the year when His Reverence, the Bishop of Mon-
> terey is on his tour of confirmation, and the California chil-
> dren are put through a severe course on the "doctrine" by their
> mothers and the parish priests, of which there are some 20

[16]Maynard J. Geiger, O.F.M., "The Apostolic College of Our Lady of Sorrows,
Santa Barbara, California," *Provincial Annals XV* (April, 1953), 74.

[17]Taken from the Register of Baptisms, Vol. I at Watsonville.

filling the seats of the old padres between Santa Cruz and San Diego.[18]

Amat was no less efficient than his predecessor and for administrative purposes, he divided the diocese into twenty districts, or areas with resident pastors. Using these parishes as centers, the limited number of priests could handle upwards of forty-five additional missionary stations or chapels over the vast expanse of the diocese. Even with this minute attention to detail, Amat foresaw the eventual necessity of forming a new jurisdiction in the northern part of his territory. Speaking, for instance, of Pajaro Valley, the bishop commented in 1866 that "within a few years another Bishop will certainly be established and form a new diocese."[19]

THE INDIAN MISSIONS

The Indians of California had been pretty much ground to pieces between the Spanish Conquest from the south up the coast, and the Anglos from the east and north across the mountains and over the desert. The pitiful condition of these wretched people has been described as the result of fierce attack in which "never before in history has a people been swept away with such terrible swiftness."[20] The normally peaceful attitude of the California native made him an easy prey to the greed of unscrupulous exploiters, a fact which accounts for their almost total lack of resistence to the seizure of their territory.

That depravity had ruined even the lives of the state's 15,000 Christian Indians[21] was noted in an account penned

[18]Quoted from the San Francisco *Bulletin*, July 15, 1865.

[19]AALA, Thaddeus Amat to Stephen Ryan, Los Angeles, March 15, 1866.

[20]A report to the Government submitted in 1877 by Stephen Powers. Quoted in Carey McWilliams, *op. cit.*, p. 41.

[21]This figure is based on estimates made in 1848. Cf. SBMA, Jose de la Guerra to John Hughes, Santa Barbara, April 18, 1849. Quoted in Joseph A. Thompson, O.F.M., *op. cit.*, p. 223.

from Los Angeles shortly after the entry of California into the Union:

> Poor Indians of California, how abandoned they are and how deplorable is their lot. Contact with civilization daily ruins their race more and more, particularly because of that great agent of destruction which is called whiskey. There are whites who kill Indians just to try their pistols. Almost every week our little village witnesses from eight to ten murders; but it is during the night between Saturday and Sunday when the most abominable crimes are committed. Many times I have had to hear the confessions of same of these mortally wounded victims.[22]

From the outset, Amat was deeply concerned about the natives, their poor living conditions, their maltreatment and most of all their spiritual direction which he acknowledged had often been overlooked. He told one of his correspondents that

> I have already taken steps toward obtaining the establishment of a religious community, either in San Luis Rey or in some other point more central to the Indians, whose object would be to attend to the civilization of the same; and another of the Sisters of Charity to perform the same duty toward the Indian females; the only means by which, in my estimation, we can effect a real and lasting good, especially if we can obtain assistance from the Superintendent for I must confess, that I feel myself unable to perfect this. . .[23]

Bishop Amat meanwhile had been asked by an agent of the United States Government for Indian Affairs for several priests to take charge of the 3,000 natives living around the San Luis Rey area. Knowing something of the history of California and the successes of the Franciscans in that highly specialized work, Amat suggested the project to the

[22]Edmond Venisse to n.n., Copiapo, Chile, June 20, 1856. Quoted in *Annales de la Propagation de la Foi* (Paris, 1858), p. 62.

[23]AALA, Thaddeus Amat to George Fisher, Santa Barbara, October 10, 1856.

friars at Santa Barbara for their consideration. His proposal was declined though and it was sometime before he could fill the need of the southern part of his diocese. Those natives living in and around San Luis Rey had, at least, nominal homes, something which could not be said of the other areas of the state. In one report it was pointed out that,

> To the Missions they can never go again, with hope of finding a home. The successors of the Fathers are there, for a priest is stationed at all except two, I believe. Any Sunday a few Indians may still be seen near the altar, summoned by the chimes that once pealed over a smiling multitude gathered for worship or the harmless diversions wherein their happy hours passed away. The rest linger there in their straggling huts of brush or tile, trying to get a meagre subsistence out of the small patches not yet taken up by the whites—ill clothed, in filth and wretchedness, without food half the year, save what is stolen.[24]

Commenting on the natives of Los Angeles, John Bartlett said he observed more Indians "about this place than any part of California" he had visited. "They were chiefly Mission Indians, that is those who had been connected with the missions, and derived their support from them until the suppression of those establishments."[25] Some thought, however, that regression to the earlier program was not the answer. And even Wilson later noted in his official report, "there are many well-meaning men, I know, who favor the idea of restoring them (the Indians) to the Missions—a knowledge of the country forbids the idea: the measure is impracticable."[26]

Nonetheless, an act of Congress on March 3, 1853, authorized the gathering of Indians into reservations and the

[24]"The B. D. Wilson Report," *Indians of Southern California in 1852* (San Marino, 1952), p. 25. Edited by John W. Caughy.

[25]*Personal Narrative* (New York, 1854), II, 82.

[26]"The B. D. Wilson Report," *op. cit.*, p. 41.

"United States Government found it imperative for saving the very lives of the surviving Indians to adopt the methods of the Franciscan friars, the very mission system which Father Junipero Serra and his brethren wisely introduced in 1770 for saving the souls of the natives."[27] Of course there were differences in the two systems; under mission rule, the natives were treated as children which was never the case on the Federal Reservations where the Indians were regarded as mere orphans and treated accordingly.

Establishment of reservations did not solve all or even a majority of the Indians' problems. That they were frequently ill-cared for by government officials can hardly be denied. Father Anthony Ubach at San Diego reported in 1873 that

> . . . I have been seven years in this place and therefore amongst them as they form a large part of my congregation and during all this period of time, no Indian Agent or Commissioner has even come down among them to see how they get along.[28]

Ubach's plea for honest and capable agents was based on the practical contention that "many thousands of dollars would be saved to the National Government if good honorable men would be appointed as its Indian Agents."

When the question of governmental assistance came up for reappraisal in 1875, a long report was addressed by a special commissioner to the Department of the Interior urging governmental action to avert utter starvation from the neglected charges. Credit in the report was given to what little Catholic missionary activity had been possible, and the commissioner freely stated that "it is an undeniable fact that to this day the Roman Catholic priests have a

[27]*Messages and Documents,* 33rd Congress, 1st Session, Senate Document No. 1., 1853-1854, Part I, p. 476.

[28]AALA, Anthony Ubach to Thaddeus Amat, San Diego, July 27, 1873.

strong influence over the Mission Indians, which influence might be exerted for their benefit if the Government would do its duty by the Indians."[29] Obviously then, the Church was still a vital part of the native culture even though it was not often able to provide as much material assistance as might have been desired.

And certainly if the Church found itself unable to lighten the blows of secular indifference toward the California natives, the cause cannot be placed at the feet of the Bishop of Monterey-Los Angeles. Lack of personnel, paucity of funds and generalized apathy on the part of the state's white population combined to make this aspect of Amat's episcopate something less than a total success. Another generation would carry on this noble work in the mid-1870's when the Bureau of Catholic Indian Missions was set up in Washington to coordinate Catholic endeavors in this field on a national level.

[29]Archives of the Bureau of Catholic Indian Missions, Charles A. Wetmore to E. P. Smith, Washington, January 9, 1875.

Thaddeus Amat was baptized in the Iglesia del Nuestra Señora del Pino, Barcelona.

(Mumbru)

*The Eglise et Seminaire des Carmes in Paris was the scene of Amat's
ordination to the priesthood.*

(Photomecaniques)

The Very Reverend Thaddeus Amat was Rector of Saint Charles Seminary in Philadelphia when the institution was located at Eighteenth and Race Street .

(Jennings)

The private oratory of the old Urban College of Propaganda Fide was the place of Amat's consecration to the bishopric.

(Debevec)

Document attesting to the bestowal of the relics of Saint Vibiana on Bishop Amat by Pius IX, May 10, 1854.

(AALA)

Formal opening of the First Vatican Council, December 8, 1869.

(Felici)

TRATADO
SOBRE EL MATRIMONIO,

SEGUN LA DOCTRINA Y DISCIPLINA

DE LA

IGLESIA CATÓLICA,

ESCRITO EN INGLÉS

por el Ilmo. y Rmo. Sr. D. Tadeo Amat,

de la Congregacion de la Mision,

Obispo de Monterey y Los Ángeles (California);

TRADUCIDO DEL INGLÉS AL ESPAÑOL POR EL MISMO AUTOR,

y aumentado con algunas notas, con los títulos de materias, y un índice
para mayor inteligencia de los lectores.

———◆———

Con aprobacion del Ordinario.

BARCELONA:

IMPRENTA DEL HEREDERO DE D. PABLO RIERA,

calle de Robador, núm. 24 y 26.

1867.

Spanish translation of Amat's Tract on Matrimony.

(AALA)

The Iglesia de San Miguel del Puerto in Barcelona was used as the model for Saint Vibiana's Cathedral in Los Angeles. This view was taken in 1876.

Saint Vibiana's Cathedral in 1876.

(AALA)

Interior view of Saint Vibiana's Cathedral in the 1880's.

The relics of Saint Vibiana are enshrined in an ornate silver reliquary over the main altar of the Cathedral bearing her name.

(Hylan)

With the deepest grief we announce to you
the death of our Most Worthy Bishop, the

R. R. Thaddeus Amat,

which occurred in this city on Sunday, May
12th. at one o'clock a. m. at the age of 67
years, 4 months and 13 days.

    We beg of you to remember him in your
prayers and respectfully invite you to his funeral,
which will take place on Tuesday, May 14th.
at 10 a. m.

    The funeral cortege will start at said hour
from the Church of Our Lady of Los Angeles,
for the Cathedral on Main St.

         † FRANCISCO MORA, Bishop,
         PEDRO VERDAGUER, Pbro.
         MIGUEL DURAN   "
         MIGUEL RUBI, C. M.
         JOAQUIN AMAT, Nephew.

Los Angeles, May 13th., 1878.

Death notice of the Right Reverend Thaddeus Amat, C.M.
(AALA)

Several days after his death, the remains of Bishop Thaddeus Amat were placed in the vault beneath the main altar of Saint Vibiana's Cathedral.

(Oberbeck)

ILLVSTRISSIMVS AC REVERENDISSIMVS D.D.

THADDEVS AMAT ET BRVSI, C. M.

NATVS BARCINONE IN HISPANIA DIE 31 DECEMBRIS A.D. 1811
VOTA PRIVATA EMISIT IN CONGREGATIONE MISSIONIS 16 IANVARII ANNO 1834
SACERDOTIO AVCTVS 23 DECEMBRIS ANNO 1837
EPISCOPVS MONEREYENSIS NOMINATVS 29 IVLII ANNO 1853
ROMAE CONSECRATVS IN COLLEGIO DE PROPAGANDA FIDE
12 MARTII ANNO 1854
TRANSLATVS AD DIOECESIM MONEREYENSIS ET ANGELORVM
3 IVLII ANNO 1859
OBIIT IN CIVITATE ANGELORVM 12 MAII ANNO 1878
SEPVLTVS IN ECCLESIA CATHEDRALI SANCTAE VIBIANAE
14. MAII ANNO 1878
REPORTATVS IN MAVSOLEVM CALVARIAE
5 DECEMBRIS ANNO 1962

On November 30, 1962, His Eminence, James Francis Cardinal Mc-Intyre directed the remains of the Right Reverend Thaddeus Amat, C.M., removed to Bishop's Crypt at Calvary Mausoleum.

(Oberbeck)

112

EXHORTACION

PASTORAL

QUE EL IL.ᴹᴼ S.ᴿ D. TADEO AMAT,

OBISPO DE MONTEREY,

DIRIGE

A LOS FIELES DE SU DIOCESIS.

Non sumus sicut plurimi adulterantes verbum Dei :
sed ex sinceritate, sed sicut ex Deo, coram Deo, in
Christo loquimur.
No somos falsificadores de la palabra de Dios, como
muchos : mas hablamos en Cristo con sinceridad, como
de parte de Dios, delante de Dios.
       S. Pablo en su segunda carta a los Co-
rinthios, cap. 2, ver. 17.
Et quicumque hanc regulam secuti fuerint: pax
super illos, et misericordia.
Y todos los que siguieren esta regla, paz sobre
ellos y misericordia.
       S. Pablo en su carta a los Galatas,
cap. 6, ver. 16.

LOS ANGELES.
IMPRESO EN LA OFICINA DEL "SOUTHERN CALIFORNIAN."

1856.

*Title page of Amat's pastoral of December 28, 1855, one of the first
pamphlets printed in Los Angeles.*

(Reproduced from copy in the Huntington Library)

113

CHAPTER SIX

RELIGIOUS AND EDUCATIONAL FOUNDATIONS

THE DAUGHTERS OF CHARITY

Most of the immigrants to California in the Gold-Rush Days were young. Nor were there great numbers of women in the early years. In the mining districts, for example, only 2% of the population was female while the number of women in the rest of the state probably did not exceed 8%. Hence children, what few there were, provided little concern from a social point of view because of their very scarcity. It was not uncommon, however, to see orphans scattered throughout the area, children whose parents were either lost at sea or killed in the cholera epidemics. The annals of San Francisco note that the fatherless and motherless children, though few in number, were left "to be tossed about in this great maelstrom of passion"[1] without any apparent concern by the city's populace. However, the problem did not go altogether unnoticed and by August of 1852, five Daughters of Charity had been brought to San Francisco by Father John Maginnis and they soon had in operation the Roman Catholic Orphanage of that city.

Concern for the welfare of its youngsters was voiced in the southland too. As early as 1851, "public sentiment was

---

[1]Quoted in Mary Stanton, "Institutional Care of California Children, 1769-1925," *Academy Scrapbook* II (January 1952), 226-227.

already aroused on the possibility of obtaining a group of Sisters of Mercy to take up educational work there, provided their material needs were suitably met."[2] The local newspaper declared that such an establishment "would confer more real benefit on this community than any other single measure."[3] But it was to be another four years before an establishment could be made.

Soon after his consecration, Bishop Amat must have received word about the needs of Los Angeles for almost immediately he set out on a quest for nuns. Uppermost in his mind, obviously, was a foundation of the Daughters of Charity with whom he had worked throughout his life. So confident was the bishop about obtaining the Daughters that he had little doubt that their superiors would agree to his request for a California establishment. On December 23, 1853 he pleaded for funds from Propagation de la Foi "to help defray the travelling expenses of the nuns to California."[4] He went to France the following September but later admitted to the Prefect of Propaganda Fide that "they have no Sisters to give me."[5]

When it became clear that he would not be able to secure religious in Europe, Amat considered the possibility of obtaining nuns from the recently affiliated Daughters of Charity at Emmitsburg, Maryland. Writing to the Very Reverend Francis Burlando, C.M., American Director of the Daughters, Amat notes that

> I shall leave Havre with four novices for our Congregation, three of my clergymen and three Postulants for the Sisterhood as I could not get Sisters either in France or in Spain owing

[2]Henry Winifred Splitter, "Los Angeles Educational Beginnings," Southern California Historical Society *Quarterly* XXXIII (June, 1951), 103.

[3]Los Angeles *Star*, July 12, 1851.

[4]AALA, Thaddeus Amat to Berard Des Glajeux, Rome, December 23, 1853.

[5]AALA, Thaddeus Amat to Cardinal Barnabo, Marseille, September 16, 1854.

to the few number they have for the present establishments. I took three young ladies in Spain[6] to be Sisters, and the Council of the Sisters at Paris has decided they will invest the Sisters at San Francisco and they will be formed there for a while to come after to Monterey.

The bishop further outlined his plans of bringing the three postulants to Emmitsburg's Novitiate for several weeks to familiarize them with the American way of life and the English language. Amat asked Burlando for three additional nuns to accompany him to San Francisco noting that "I shall not leave Emmitsburg without them . . . I must have them."[7]

The small group sailed on May 19th for the United States and arrived in New York in about four weeks. Amat sent the novices and postulants to Emmitsburg and it was envisioned that Father Hugh Gallagher would accompany the women on to San Francisco when their training period was completed.[8] Journeying through Perryville to Saint Louis, one newspaper printed his observations in its columns.

Informed of the destitute state of my diocese . . . I directed my views to establish in Monterey[9] the Sisters of Charity, to take care of all the unfortunate human beings many of whom found their misery where they expected to find plenty of gold.[10]

Delayed for some weeks in the east on business, Amat eventually decided to return to Emmitsburg and personally conduct the Sisters to California.

On October 20, 1855 Amat and his party sailed from New York to the Isthmus at Aspinwall. Their voyage was

---

[6]Amat obtained the postulants at Barcelona's Juventudes de la Medella Milagrosa.

[7]AALA, Thaddeus Amat to Francis Burlando, Paris, May 7, 1855.

[8]AALA, Thaddeus Amat to Francis Burlando, Pittsburg, June 24, 1855.

[9]The bishop is referring to his diocese, not the city.

[10]The *Leader*, July 21, 1855.

remarkably prosperous and one nun notes that there was "not even a white cap on the water."[11] Early on the morning of Wednesday, November 14th, the Pacific Mail Company's steamship, *John C. Stephens*, reached her wharf at San Francisco after a two-week journey from Panama. The Sisters were warmly welcomed by their confreres at San Francisco who had been in the Bay City for almost three years.

LOS ANGELES ORPHANAGE

Amat's proposal to open an orphanage in Los Angeles met with the immediate approval of that city's civic leaders and a meeting was called for Thursday, December 16th, 1855 to work out the necessary details for such an undertaking. The first order of business was the raising of funds to house the nuns who would staff the institution and in this regard a committee was formed to canvass the city for subscriptions. Prominent among those participating in the preparations was John G. Downey who was to become California's Governor five years later.[12] A native of Ireland and a life-long Catholic, Downey had operated the only drug- store between San Francisco and San Diego and by 1855 was among the largest property-holders in the city. Downey's interest in the project did much to further the cause and was only one of a long series of examples of his charitable interests.[13]

Chosen to lead the establishment of Sisters in Los Angeles was Sister Mary Scholastica Logsdon, a native of Maryland who had been associated in her childhood with another California pioneer, J. De Barth Shorb. A member

---

[11]AALA, n.n. to Charles Conroy, Saint Joseph, Missouri, September 17, 1951.

[12]I.e. on January 4, 1860.

[13]Cf. Hubert H. Bancroft, *Chronicles of the Builders* (San Francisco, 1892), II, 128.

of the Daughters of Charity since 1839, she was eminently qualified for the task for, as one historian noted,

> Every pioneer knows how far away California seemed in those days when no railway stretched connecting bands of steel across the great continent; when one heard strange and vague reports of the primitive life of the Far West; when "Prairie Schooners" led one through the terrors of Indian attack "across the plains," or a long voyage by steamer brought one a wearisome journey via the Isthmus of Panama. I repeat, it required a staunch heart to venture into this unknown world, and, above all, it required a courage inspired by the faith of Sister Scholastica, for women to undertake this journey that they might minister to those in need.[14]

Sister Scholastica and her five companions disembarked in San Francisco in November of 1855 and delayed in the Bay City only long enough for the bishop to arrange for their housing at Los Angeles. They reached the southland "sooner than was expected, for the Bishop who left us in San Francisco, wrote for us to come down in the next steamer which he thought would leave at a later date; but we hurried off taking passage on the next boat."[15] Their arrival at San Pedro on the coastwise ship *Sea Bird* was duly recorded by the local press:

> Six Sisters of Charity arrived in this city last Saturday, January 6, 1856 . . . three are from the United States and three from Spain, consequently, both languages will be taught in school.[16]

The missionary activity which the Daughters of Charity were to inaugurate began with anything but solemnity as can be seen by a description of their first impressions:

[14]W. H. Workman, "Sister Scholastica," *Historical Society of Southern California Annual* V (1902), 257.

[15]Archives of Maryvale (hereafter referred to as AM), Extract from the "Life of Sister Scholastica Logsdon," Annals, p. 1.

[16]*El Clamor Publico*, January 12, 1856.

The rumbling of the heavy Phineas Banning stagecoach, the pounding of the horses' hoofs, the barking of dogs, and finally, the boom of the town's cannon—such were the heralds announcing the arrival in Southern California of the first Daughters of Charity of St. Vincent de Paul. The day, January 6, 1856, was uneventful in the Los Angeles pueblo of less than nine thousand people save for the advent of these six blue-clad Sisters from Emmitsburg, Maryland.

The coachman reined the horses to a stop and quickly jumped down to open the door. Six Daughters of Charity emerged, bearing the meagre belongings with which they had shared the bumpy ten-hour ride from San Pedro. The leader of the little band, Sister Mary Scholastica Logsdon, and her companions, Sisters: Ann Gillen, Clara Sisnero, Angelita Mumbardo, Marie Corsina, and Francisca Fernandez, gazed wonderingly and not a little skeptically at their new environment. It was late afternoon. The few Indians and Spaniards on the dusty street eyed the newcomers with curiosity. One politely escorted them to the Mission Church, where they were kindly received by the good priest, Father Anacletus.[17]

News of their arrival was quickly sent to Bishop Amat who was on confirmation tour at San Gabriel. A close friend of the bishop's, Don Ignacio del Valle, former mayor or alcalde of Los Angeles, turned over his home to the sisters and "received us as if we were angels." The committee had confined itself to fund raising and up to this point had made no specific plans for a definite house for the nuns, thinking it wiser to let them select a place which satisfied their personal wants and needs.

When we arrived at Los Angeles, the house was not purchased, as the gentlemen commissioned to attend to the matter, awaited the Bishop's coming to determine which would be most suitable to the Sisters.[18]

[17]*One Hundred Years of Service* (Los Angeles, 1956), p. 12.
[18]AM, Extract, p. 2.

There were several alternatives for housing the sisters and when Amat returned two days later, a number of places were inspected. One respected member of the small community noted in his diary that his wife,

Emily took much interest in the introduction of the Sisters of Saint Vincent into this city. She and I accompanied them, after their arrival, in their rounds among the different houses offered for their selection. She encouraged them in what their own good taste and sagacity dictated, in the places they were urged to accept and their final choice of the beautiful grounds of Hon. B. D. Wilson.[19]

Their selection of the twelve acre orchard and vineyard surrounding the lovely home of Benjamin David Wilson (Don Benito!) was a wise one. The home was one of the "first frame buildings in El Pueblo and it faced the Alameda where Macy Street now intersects Alameda."

In her memoirs, Sister Scholastica notes that,

The place was purchased at once, and four days after we were conducted to our new home where, with our dear orphans we are quite comfortable. We have an excellent gardener and in a few days we shall have a woman to cook for us.[20]

The civic leaders saw in the advent of the Sisters the beginnings of a new development in education and community service. As one historian observed: ". . . immediately they formed an important adjunct to the Church in matters pertaining to religion, charity and education."[21] Another observer noted that, "when their wooden building was erected, on the site where the Union Station now stands, the first institute and Orphan Asylum south of San Francisco was opened."[22]

---

[19]Benjamin J. Hayes, op. cit., p. 172.
[20]AM, Extract, p. 2. The house cost $8,000.
[21]Harris Newmark, op. cit., p. 189.
[22]Mary Stanton, "The Development of Institutional Care of Children in California from 1769 to 1925," The Social Service Review (September, 1951), p. 323.

The Daughters opened their day school and home for orphans with seven youngsters, a small number but one which was destined to grow as the years moved on. By June 7, 1856, there were 120 sons and daughters of the first families of Los Angeles, Catholic, Protestant and Jew and the Sisters seemed well satisfied in their new surroundings in spite of the obvious disadvantages which were described by one writer in most unattractive terms:

> It was to a primitive town that the Sisters came, primitive in society, business and government. Its three thousand inhabitants had among them many restless and reckless characters, disgruntled Mexicans and depraved Indians, whose number was augmented by criminals driven from the north by the vigilantes.[23]

Annual Orphan Fairs were inaugurated by the nuns, the first of which was held in October of 1857. One chronicler notes that,

> Socially, for many years, the biggest events were the fairs that were given for the support of the Sisters of Charity and their good work. The date of the fairs was always set for "steamer day," which meant the day that the boat came in from San Francisco.[24]

With the proceeds from their annual Fairs, the Sisters were able to remain at their posts and in later years became the most respected religious community in all the southland.

SISTERS AT SANTA BARBARA

In May of 1856, Amat wrote to Burlando for an additional "twenty sisters for five establishments . . . in the most important places of the Diocese."[25] That fall the first

---

[23]William E. North, *Catholic Education in Southern California* (Washington, 1930), p. 126.

[24]Boyle Workman, *op. cit.*, p. 43.

[25]AALA, Thaddeus Amat to Francis Burlando, Santa Cruz, May 30, 1856.

extension of the Daughters took place when a second group of nuns left Emmitsburg "to open a school where English could be taught in Santa Barbara in the new State of California."[26] Tragedy struck in Panama where one of the five nuns succumbed to tropical fever. The four remaining Sisters went on to San Francisco, arriving ultimately at Santa Barbara on December 28th where they were eagerly received by Father James Vila.

Through the kindness of F. J. Maguire, the Sisters were lodged temporarily in the historic adobe on State Street at Carillo reputed to have served at one time as the headquarters of General John C. Fremont, until their school was completed. Within a short time after its opening at Las Cienequitas on January 3, 1857 neglected and orphaned Indian youngsters were gathered in from the area on oxcarts, wagons, donkeys, ponies and on foot to attend the first English speaking school in the area, Saint Vincent's Institution. The original purpose of the bishop was to provide the security of a home and a school for those children between the ages of three and sixteen. From the very beginning, the foundation was successful and received the utmost cooperation from the inhabitants of Santa Barbara where the school was relocated in January of 1858.

As the oldest charitable institution in Santa Barbara, Saint Vincent's school struggled along for the next seventeen years. In 1873 a larger piece of land was acquired and work commenced on a two story brick edifice. Completed the next year, the new building burned to the ground within a few months. It was rebuilt and by November of 1874 the Sisters were able to move into their new quarters.

[26]Mary Stanton, "Institutional Care of California Children, 1769-1925," *Academy Scrapbook*, II (January, 1952), 227-228.

LOS ANGELES INFIRMARY

A third contingent of Daughters of Charity arrived in San Francisco on January 6, 1858 to staff the southland's new "county hospital." There had been no such facilities in Los Angeles during the 1850's and it was only on May 29, 1858 that the city witnessed the opening of its first medical dispensary in the home of Don Cristobal Aguilar, a small adobe building at Bath and Alameda streets near the Plaza. The Sisters subsequently purchased property from Don Luis Arenas on Chavez Lane in the early 1860's and moved into the two story building. There was no water in the four room house and all linen had to be carried to the river bank to be washed. Nonetheless the Daughters were ready to announce on June 21st of 1869 that their Los Angeles Infirmary had been incorporated.

> Sisters of Charity would respectfully announce to the suffering members of the community, that, having completed a large, commodious, well ventilated building for the use of the County Patients, they can now accommodate a number of both male and female Patients with Private Rooms, where they shall receive the care and attentive solicitude of the devoted Sisters.[27]

Their new location, the gift of Prudent Beaudry, was on Sunset Boulevard near the street bearing the donor's name.[28]

OTHER FOUNDATIONS

In 1861 Father Anthony Ubach entreated the nuns to open an orphanage and school at San Juan Bautista.[29] The

[27]Los Angeles *Star*, October 2, 1869.

[28]Boyle Workman, *op. cit.*, p. 59.

[29]Zephryin Engelhardt, O.F.M., *Mission San Juan Bautista* (San Francisco, 1931), p. 107.

tiny village had grown to some importance as the site of an exchange station on the route between San Francisco and Los Angeles and needed the services of the sisters for its increased population. Classes were held in the long room back of the sacristies, while the Sisters themselves occupied the cloister or monastery of the mission.[30] As many as 120 day pupils and thirty-five orphans were attached to the mission at one time.

The financially precarious condition of the Diocese of Monterey-Los Angeles prevented a more rapid growth of its educational program. In 1861 the resourceful Zachariah Montgomery had introduced the first of many bills in the state legislature[31] to provide that schools with a minimum of thirty children and established by parents or guardians be given the right to qualify as public schools, with religious instruction and catechism taught as an appendage but controlled by the parents. Although subsequently one unfriendly source stated that there was "imminent danger of its passage," the bill was roundly defeated in spite of the fact that public schools would not begin flourishing for some years in California.[32] Regardless of this setback, however, the Daughters of Charity managed to set up an orphanage and school for girls at Santa Cruz in 1862. It was felt that the town's growth, which rated for it a charter from the state in 1866, warranted a school and although the town was not located on one of the main arteries of trade, its remarkably quick expansion would seem to have justified the action. An old adobe building, formerly the

---

[30]Amat had obtained four additional Spanish nuns from Europe in 1860 and with these was able to exchange personnel with Emmitsburg.

[31]John Sweet, *History of the Public School System of California* (San Francisco, 1876), p. 31.

[32]Cf. James T. Booth, *Church Educational Problems in the State of California* (Rome, 1960) for the background.

Eagle Hotel, which had belonged to the early mission, served as the first school house, and three sisters were allotted for the new foundation which brought joy to the heart of all those concerned for the youngsters of the area.

Communications with Paris and Emmitsburg were anything but rapid and Bishop Amat seems to have wanted a separate province of the Daughters of Charity set up in the west at an early date. His intentions in that regard were apparently misunderstood as an attempt to establish his own diocesan community and he was forced to reiterate to Burlando that "I would send them away from my diocese if they would attempt to be independent." Amat went on to point out that "it will be necessary, in the course of time, to have in California a novitiate of the Sisters of Charity, and to form out of it a new Province, as has been done in Mexico. . . ." Vocations were exceedingly scarce and Amat believed "you will not get any young lady from this . . . [area] to make her Novitiate either in Emmitsburg or in Mexico."[33]

The matter was submitted at Paris to the Superior General and his council late the next year and on November 29, 1858 the request was granted.[34] A seminary (or novitiate) was opened at Los Angeles Orphanage in May of 1861 and lasted until October of 1870 when it was closed for lack of financial means and a dearth of vocations.

IMMACULATE HEART SISTERS

Bishop Amat's disappointment at not obtaining larger numbers of Daughters of Charity forced him to look elsewhere for additional religious women to fill the growing needs of California. Attention soon focused on his na-

[33]AALA, Thaddeus Amat to Francis Burlando, Santa Cruz, May 30, 1856.
[34]AMM, "Registre. . . .," II, 261.

tive Catalonia and the Congregacion de las Hijas del Ssmo. e Inmado. Corazon de Maria. The small town of Olot had witnessed the foundation of this community on July 2, 1848 when Canon Joaquin Masmitja gathered together a congregation to engage in catechetical instruction to youngsters not able to obtain formal schooling.

On his way to the First Vatican Council in November of 1869,[35] the bishop approached Canon Masmitja on the subject pointing out the tremendous need for sisters in the vast California mission. Amat felt confidant that with a beginning of five or six women, augmented in time by native volunteers, the tide of secularism in the Golden State could be turned in the Church's favor. Masmitja was not at first too impressed by the proposal and Amat went on to Rome. There he contacted Archbishop Anthony Claret about his plans and found in the future saint a true friend. Claret was enthusiastic about the American apostolate and was known to have stated that were it not that "I am an old man . . . I would fly there myself." He even went so far as to prophesy that America "in the near future will give more saints to heaven than all Europe."[36]

Having lent encouragement to Masmitja's foundation some twenty-five years earlier, Claret was able to influence the canon to act favorably on Amat's plea. By the middle of February, 1870 ten nuns were preparing to leave for California and spending their time learning English at Gerona. Amat had hoped to arrive at Olot in September but was prevented from doing so by the outbreak of the Franco-Prussian War.[37]

[35]Tomas Noguer y Musqueras, *Biografia . . . D. Joaquin Masmitja y de Puig* (Gerona, 1952), p. 347.

[36]Quoted in Sister Marietta, I.H.M., "The Sisters of the Immaculate Heart of Mary," (Los Angeles, 1948), p. 13.

[37]Tomas Noguer, *op. cit.,* p. 351.

The bishop returned to the United States and waited until the next July when he sent his vicar general, Father Francis Mora to bring the sisters from Olot. The contingent of ten nuns and Father Mora left Gerona, appropriately enough, on the feast of Our Lady of the Angels and went directly to Liverpool and then on to New York and San Francisco where they arrived on the 31st of August.[38]

Records of the Immaculate Heart community reveal that

> . . . on the third day of September (1871) they were accompanied to Gilroy by the Most Illustrious Bishop Amat, who left them in the house there, that is four choir sisters, and one of obedience and the other five were taken to San Juan Bautista.[39]

The convent at Gilroy, about a mile from the city on land adjacent to Saint Mary's Church, was destined for the novitiate. In 1873 the novitiate was moved to San Juan Bautista and in 1878 to San Luis Obispo. The probable motive for placing five of the nuns at San Juan Bautista instead of Los Angeles as previously agreed, "was Father Cyprian Rubio's interest in the re-establishment of the San Juan Bautista Orphanage which had been abandoned about 1869 by the Daughters of Charity"[40] because of a misunderstanding with Rubio. In any event school opened again on September 11, 1871 and carried on the work of the Daughters for another generation. The sisters supported their orphanage through contributions of money, food and other supplies and by fees charged from the day

[38]Mariano Aguilar, *Historia de la Congregacion de las Hijas del Ssmo e Inmado Corazon de Maria,* (Barcelona, 1909), p. 199.

[39]AALA, Legal statement, Reply to the Reverend Hieronymous Baillo, Los Angeles, n.d., p. 5.

[40]Sister M. Reginald Baggot, I.H.M., "The California Institute of the Sisters of the Most Holy and Immaculate Heart of the Blessed Virgin Mary," (Los Angeles, 1937), p. 17.

school. A boarding institution functioned briefly but was later closed at the behest of Bishop Mora.

The sisters' convent at Gilroy stood in the middle of an uncultivated, treeless fifteen acre oasis. Crammed within the two-story frame building were two classrooms, two music rooms, several poorly lighted dormitories and a kitchen and dining room. An academy and a private day school soon opened at Gilroy with an enrollment of upwards of thirty-five pupils. Boarding accommodations were quickly readied and the increase in students continued despite the distance from town.

A block of land in San Luis Obispo had been given to the diocese in 1857 by Don Dolores Herrera for a convent. After clearing title to the land in 1872, the bishop heeded pleas from the town's inhabitants and allowed a school to be opened there. Several years passed and on August 2, 1876 the foundation was taken over by the sisters under the title of Immaculate Heart Academy. The infant school received hearty support from all sides and one glowing newspaper reporter noted in the year that "the institution is not second to any similar one in the state."[41]

CHURCH EDUCATIONAL PROBLEMS IN CALIFORNIA

There had been very little of an educational nature going on when California came into the Union in 1850. But the expanding population in the subsequent five years witnessed the alloting of public funds to all schools, denominational and otherwise, so much so that between 1850 and 1855 all education in the state, except that in San Francisco, was under church direction. However, as the Legislature began to fill up with members born in states where the ideas of Horace Mann were in the ascendency, the attitude towards private schools quickly changed.

[41]San Luis Obispo *Tribune,* December 23, 1876.

Sincere advocates of a state monopoly in educational affairs gradually found themselves allied with those critics of the Church who characterized the role of Catholic schools as propaganda mills of "popish plots." One such "progressive thinker" was D. R. Ashley of Monterey who led a campaign in the Legislature to deny public funds to sectarian schools. Ashley received endorsement from several sources, one of which was the public press:

> Everyone knows that as all denominations stand related to the great question of public schools, the only motive for such an act is to pander to the Catholic population who are unwilling to have their children receive an American popular education . . . They dare not have their children mingle freely with freeborn Americans.[42]

The Ashley bill, as passed into law on May 3, 1855, provided that "no portion of the Common School Fund . . . nor of the moneys raised by the State tax or specially appropriated for the support of the common schools shall be diverted to any other object or purpose."[43] Passage of the bill was due, in no small measure, to Know Nothingism which was then strong, especially in Northern California.

In the Diocese of Monterey, already in shaky financial condition, the Ashley Bill tended to stall the growth of a diocesan school system. Almost all the state's Protestant elementary schools "closed their doors for lack of funds or became secularized public schools and the Catholic schools are fighting to make ends meet to remain open."[44]

Early in 1861, Archbishop Alemany and Bishop Amat were among fifty-four ministers to sign a petition seeking revisions to the Ashley Bill. This action was carried for-

[42]The *Pacific*, May 4, 1855.

[43]*Statutes* of 1855, Sec. 23, p. 229.

[44]Mark J. Hurley, *Church-State Relationships in Education in California* (Washington, 1948), p. 29.

ward by Zachariah Montgomery who, on March 29th, introduced legislation to grant public funds for religious schools on a *pro rata* basis. His bill provided that "no religion is to be taught unless such be the will of said parents . . . and in no event shall religious instruction lessen the five hours of secular education."[45] But pitted against such outspoken opponents as John Swett and John Conness who maintained that the proposal "was imported . . . by the advocates of Catholicism and is in direct antagonism to our American system of common schools,"[46] Montgomery's efforts were eventually frustrated. One authority observed that the "bill was identified as strictly Catholic stratagem and Protestantism and the common schools were again identified as the same thing."[47]

The defeat of Montgomery's bill was a major set-back for private education since the "Catholic schools had for a long time shared in the public school funds."[48] The new legislation received this editorial comment from San Francisco:

> In the new School Law passed by the last Legislature and now in force, I find the following section: 'No books, tracts or papers shall be used or introduced in any schools established under the provisions of this Act![49]

In the same paper, a question was sent to the editor asking whether this ruling prohibited the reading of the Bible at school, or if the law forbade teaching religion before or after the normal school day begins. The response indicated that the law was not explicit on these points and would probably need testing in the courts.

[45]*California State Journal* (Sacramento, 1862), p. 480.
[46]Sacramento Daily *Union,* April 13, 1861.
[47]James T. Booth, *op. cit.,* p. 37.
[48]Richard Gabel, *Public Funds for Church and Private Schools* (Washington, 1937), p. 469.
[49]San Francisco *Chronicle,* July 5, 1855.

LOS ANGELES CATHOLIC SCHOOLS

Before the coming of the Americans, most children were educated at home or in private schools. There is no evidence of any school in Los Angeles between 1846 and 1849 a fact reflected in the illiteracy ratio for the city which passed the 60% rate.[50]

The Picpus Fathers opened a small school in Los Angeles as early as March of 1851.[51] Known only as the "Boarding and Day School at Los Angeles," there were three priests attached to the institution which limped along until the summer of 1853 when it was closed and the Fathers recalled to the Sandwich Islands. On August 10, 1856 Bishop Amat and Father Blasius Raho reopened the school in a rented adobe building under the title of Saint Vincent's College.[52] The earlier institution had benefited by a code passed on July 9, 1851 by the City Council providing a sum of about $50 per month toward "the support of any educational institution in the city, provided that all the rudiments of the English and Spanish languages be taught therein."[53] There are no extant records of the school and no indication as to how long it survived. The curtailment of public assistance by statewide legislation in 1856 greatly hampered its activities and it is believed that the small school had a very short existence. Nor is there evidence of any connection between this institution and the later college of the same name although both were under Vincentian auspices.

[50]William Warren Ferrier, *Ninety Years of Education in California* (Berkeley, 1937), p. 260.

[51]Quoted in Charles C. Conroy, "The Picpus School in Los Angeles," *Academy Scrapbook,* II (November, 1951), 165.

[52]Henry Winifred Splitter, "Los Angeles Educational Beginnings," *Academy Scrapbook,* II (December, 1951), 193.

[53]Reginald Yzendoorn, SS.CC., *op. cit.,* p. 187.

The school was revived a third time in March of 1867 when the Vincentian Fathers moved their college from the plaza to its new site on Sixth street. Bishop Amat engaged the Brothers of Saint Francis,[54] recently arrived from the Diocese of Brooklyn, to utilize the old college quarters for a small primary school. Under the title of Saint Mary's Parochial School, the insitution received little or no mention in the early chronicles because of its insignificance in relation to the larger Saint Vincent's. Under a somewhat misleading caption "Institute of the Christian Brothers," the following notice appeared in the Los Angeles *Star* announcing the school's activities:

> In the old adobe building, formerly the Lugo House, east of the Plaza, in Los Angeles, is located the School of the Christian Brothers. This institution is under the auspices of the Bishop of the Catholic Church and is immediately presided over by two Franciscan monks [*sic*]. It affords gratuitous education to male children of all ages, denominations and nations, Hebrew, African, Chinese who otherwise cannot attend school for want of means.[55]

Saint Mary's continued on for about six years, sometimes referred to only as "the parochial school." Classes were taught in Spanish, still the predominate language in the southland. Local annals are silent on the longevity of Saint Mary's but it failed to appear in the Catholic Directory after 1874.

Despite the legal obstacles involved in setting up and financing a Catholic school system, Bishop Amat consistently advocated the erection of parochial educational units and even incorporated a provision along these lines into the statutes of the diocese directing pastors to "watch care-

---

[54]The Brothers had left their native Diocese of Brooklyn in 1863 without the knowledge or authorization of their ordinary.

[55]July 26, 1870.

fully over those youngsters who attend public schools. . . ."[56]

It had been Amat's desire to see a school established in every parish of the diocese, since that seemed the only practical way of educating the youngsters in their catechism. In some areas, the plan was plainly not workable but in Santa Barbara, for instance, where the bishop had lived for some years, he was especially anxious that a school be erected which he hoped would raise the uncommonly low standard of living. A college[57] for boys was, therefore, opened at the mission on March 2, 1868, in the interest of encouraging vocations to the Franciscans whose numbers were declining. In addition, the friars and Amat both knew that although the great majority of seminary students did not persevere through the entire course, it would enable those who left the college to attain a higher type of work within the community. The college functioned for about eleven years and achieved some success in providing a higher education for certain of the local youngsters, although, unfortunately, few if any vocations were realized. The purpose of the college was stated in its prospectus for 1872-1873:

> The object of this institution is to give a good English and classic education at the lowest possible cost—a want of which has long been felt in California. To cultivate the heart no less than to develop the intellect and physical powers of the students is a duty the Fathers keep constantly in mind.

The setting of the college was one of its more appealing aspects, nestled as it was on a plateau about 250 feet above the town with a beautiful view of the sea in the distance. The institution was governed by what was termed a "venerable and much-esteemed Catholic priest, once the Presi-

[56]*Constitutiones Latae et Promulgatae* (San Francisco, 1862), pp. 21-22.
[57]It was known as the Colegio Franciscano.

dent of the Catholic Missions; who has lived in the country since 1833 and is well known to the old pioneers from Sonoma to Arizona, a most unselfish kind-hearted old philosopher."[58] In the years after 1874 "it suffered from a dwindling student body and from increasing financial embarrassment"[59] and it closed its doors May 31, 1877.

[58]The venerable and much esteemed priest was Father Gonzales Rubio. Cf. San Francisco *Bulletin*, April 13, 1868.

[59]Maynard J. Geiger, O.F.M., The Franciscan Boy's College, *Academy Scrapbook*, I, 195.

Chapter Seven

CATHOLIC COLLEGIATE EDUCATION
IN SOUTHERN CALIFORNIA

THE Catholic bishop who does not think in terms of having his own seminary is the exception, for otherwise he has no secure manner of providing priests to care for his flock and to staff his diocesan institutions. There were two attempts made in the early Catholic history of Southern California to fill this need. Neither achieved the precise goal originally intended, but both made sizeable contributions to the development of Catholic life in the new ecclesiastical jurisdiction.

Formal education in California had been unknown before the arrival in 1794, of Governor Diego de Borica. Education, what little there was, remained sporadic and ill-organized for as one historian has said, the "Franciscans came to California not as schoolmen but as apostles," and in their roles as missionaries "their main concern was to awaken the soporific minds of their Indian neophytes to an appreciation of the divine, imponderable truths of Christianity."[1] Nonetheless, "every Mission was almost as much a school as a church . . . for every well developed Mission was a great industrial establishment with an industrial

[1]William E. North, *op. cit.*, p. 13.

school at the center."[2] However, with the advent of the colorful Borica, commonly referred to as the father of the public schools of California,[3] a concerted attempt was made to establish schools so that literacy might prevail in the presidios and pueblos. But the governor's constant proddings had little effect and as has been said, he bemoaned the apathy into which he too was forced to sink.[4]

In the decades between 1820 and 1840 the accomplishments were no more encouraging and educational efforts were to remain a haphazard affair until after the American conquest, with one notable exception. Manuel Micheltorena, described as a "genial gentleman who was in many ways deserving of better fortune than fate accorded him as ruler of the Californias. . . .,"[5] came to the province as governor in 1842 and had in mind the fostering of education as a training in the recognition of vocational, moral and intellectual virtues. He wasted no time in seeing that schools were opened at San Diego, Los Angeles, Santa Barbara, Monterey, San Jose, San Francisco and Sonoma, all with a specific and strict curriculum. Article 10 of his *Reglamento* prescribed that "for the patroness of these schools the Most Holy Virgin of Guadalupe shall be adopted, and her image shall be given an appropriate place in each school."[6] Micheltorena's educational activity earned for the governor the evaluation that "the chief merit of his administration was the great encouragement he gave to schools and to education." Unfortunately, this patron of learning lost his office on February 22, 1845, for his un-

[2]Herbert E. Bolton, "The Mission as a Frontier Institution," *American Historical Review*, XXIII (October, 1917), 45.

[3]Theodore H. Hittell, *History of California*, (San Francisco, 1896), II, 595.

[4]Mark J. Hurley, *op. cit.*, p. xii.

[5]Charles E. Chapman, *A History of California* (New York, 1921), p. 480.

[6]Theodore H. Hittell, *op. cit.*, II, 341.

willingness to enforce the confiscatory law directed against the mission chain.

Nonetheless, it was during Micheltorena's tenure as governor that the first diocesan seminary in the new Diocese of Both Californias was opened in 1842 in several rooms of the old mission buildings at Santa Barbara. It was only a temporary arrangement and as the number of students increased and the facilities became inadequate, Bishop Garcia Diego decided to erect a new seminary adjacent to Santa Ines Mission. Soon after submitting a formal petition for a land grant to Micheltorena, the generous governor granted the request.[7] The original grant consisted of six square leagues which was augmented several months later to include a vast tract of 35,499 acres. This was a considerable piece of land even in those days and it was officially transferred to the bishop in April of 1845, under the title *Rancho Canada de los Pinos,* or in English, the College Ranch. In a constitution,[8] drawn up by the bishop to govern the administration of the institution, the new seminary, which was also the first college in California,[9] was pledged to accept students other than those preparing for the priesthood, with a preference for orphans and the poor. Unfortunately, the seminary never developed as had been hoped and the bishop did not disguise his disappointment when he stated,

> . . . for the seminary, which with wretched means I have started, offers no hope of prosperity. The attendance is reduced to a small number of boys, whom with some hardship

[7]Zephryin Engelhardt, O.F.M., *Mission Santa Ines* (Santa Barbara, 1932), p. 51.

[8]SBMA, II, Constitutions, Santa Ines, May 4, 1844.

[9]A fact pointedly overlooked in Ferrier's study. A small college, established by William Hartnell at Mission San Carlos in 1834, was described "as the first established in California" in Yzendoorn's study.

I must clothe and feed, and the education, for want of professors and funds, cannot be as thorough as I might wish.[10]

Chief among the reasons for the seminary's failure was the extreme poverty of the Church, along with the absence of an educational tradition in California and the political unrest then prevalent.[11]

In 1850, while Father Gonzales Rubio was administrator of the diocese, the seminary was confided to the care of the Picpus Fathers,[12] then exiled from their missions in the Sandwich Islands. They altered and broadened somewhat the original purposes of the college as was indicated in the entry in the *Catholic Almanac* for 1851 which read, ". . . a college has been commenced at Santa Ines about four hundred miles from San Francisco." There was not even any mention of the seminary. Soon after Bishop Joseph Sadoc Alemany's arrival in 1851, and the transfer of the Picpus Fathers to Los Angeles, Father Eugene O'Connell, a professor at All Hallows College, Dublin, became Rector of Santa Ines College and following his tenure there was a succession of short-term superiors. When the diocese was divided in 1853, the fortunes of the seminary improved temporarily. Father Cyprian Rubio became superior and during his regime the student enrollment rose to a peak of twenty-five. Rubio used various ingenious methods to boost the enrollment, among which were advertisements in the local newspapers such as the following:

This institution, established with the object to educate youths who have some disposition for the ecclesiastical state, has offered great services to the community giving a knowledge of

---

[10]AALA, *"Libro Borrador,"* Representacion, September 27, 1843.

[11]Finbar Kenneally, O.F.M., *op. cit.,* p 6.

[12]Reginald Yzendoorn, SS.CC., *op. cit.,* p. 189.

the sciences to youths who otherwise would be deprived of the great treasure of human knowledge.[13]

However, despite the fact that parts of the ranch were under cultivation, and other areas used for the raising of cattle, the deficits continued to plague the institution, not only because of operational costs but also because of the necessity for a series of major repairs. Moreover, Santa Ines was operated jointly by Archbishop Alemany and Bishop Thaddeus Amat who frequently disagreed about administrative policies. Governor Micheltorena's grant had carried with it certain legal reservations among which was a stipulation that if and when there was a split in the original ecclesiastical jurisdiction, the college would become provincial, that is, it would serve the needs of the several diocesan divisions resulting from the split. Further, it was stated that all operating expenses would be shared on a *pro-rata* basis, that is, by all the parties involved in the divisions of the earlier jurisdiction. Hence one-fifth of these expenses were to be paid by the Vicar Apostolic of Baja California, two-fifths by the Bishop of Monterey and two-fifths by the Archbishop of San Francisco. This arrangement was certainly not an equitable one for Alemany since the majority of students at that time were from the Diocese of Monterey. Moreover, there is no evidence that the Vicar Apostolic of Baja California[14] was ever able to meet his part of this indebtedness. It was understandable, therefore, that Alemany complained to Amat that "it is your diocese that has derived the entire benefit from the

[13]*El Clamor Publico,* September 26, 1857.

[14]There are no available records of payments by the Vicar of Baja California. As a matter of fact, there is no evidence that Baja California even had a vicar before 1874. Bishop Francisco Escalante governed the area between 1856 and 1872 but his canonical status has yet to be determined. Cf. the author's *Pioneer Catholicism in the Californias* (Van Nuys, 1961), p. 16 for a brief sketch of Baja California's episcopal history.

the college in the education given in it since you were made bishop."[15] A clause in the original grant had stated, however, that the college could be discontinued with the permission of the government. And even though there had been a change of sovereignty, apparently there would have been little objection to the sale of the property on the part of the new United States government, provided a suitable buyer could be found. These legal minutiae did not at first appeal to Alemany since he thought the Church had a definite obligation to respect the obvious intentions of the Mexican governor. As he told Amat early in 1857, "I do not think the property could be retained or defended in favor of the Church if the object of the grant was not carried out."[16]

To complicate matters further, Alemany and Amat were unable to agree on a practical plan for disposing of the property should a prospective buyer be found. The archbishop insisted that the college be moved from the mission to the nearby ranch buildings of San Isidro, a mile and a half from its present location. After much delay, a temporary agreement was drawn up in the summer of 1860 between the two ordinaries which embodied the following provisions:

(1) Very Rev. J. Croke shall be the administrator of the College to be kept at San Isidro;

(2) He shall be authorized to spend what will be necessary in his judgment for fixing up for the purpose said house of San Isidro, not exceeding in such expense the sum of one thousand dollars;

(3) He shall be authorized to appoint an honest man capable of teaching the english branches and to employ a few servants indispensable for the keeping of said house;

[15]AALA, Joseph S. Alemany to Thaddeus Amat, San Francisco, May 24, 1861.
[16]AALA, Joseph S. Alemany to Thaddeus Amat, San Francisco, March 20, 1857.

(4) No expense for repairs, or other things, except to meet the above shall be incurred above three hundred dollars without the express consent of the parties or their agents;

(5) Each bishop interested shall place in the hands of V. Rev. J. Croke till proportion be better ascertained, the following sums. . . .[17]

Further, the archbishop wished to have only an elementary day school at San Isidro if and when the move became feasible. "It is clear to my mind," he told Amat, "that with due permission the college should be moved to another locality, leaving a good school for the present place."[18] But this suggestion was utterly unacceptable to Bishop Amat who promptly countered in language that left no doubt about his stand:

> I most humbly beg you, Most Rev. Sir, not to imagine that there can be a simple day school at Santa Ines. It must of necessity be a boarding school or college, for that place is still a wildernesss, and there was never, since I am here, a single day school as far as I know.[19]

Amat went on to say that, with the approval of the Holy See, he would take the cattle for his share in the college ranch. He readily acknowledged that the value of the land far exceeded that of the cattle, but he added, "I value more highly the cattle than the ranch with the obligation of keeping the college."[20]

Ultimately the proposal for a day school was abandoned by Alemany but he continued, nevertheless, to favor moving the site of the college to San Isidro, on the same property, unless a more suitable location could be found; and in the same vein he advised Amat that he would not be ac-

[17]AALA, Alemany memorandum, n.p., July 5, 1860. Reverend James Croke was a priest of the Archdiocese of San Francisco.

[18]AALA, Joseph S. Alemany to Thaddeus Amat, San Francisco, July 18, 1861.

[19]AALA, Thaddeus Amat to Joseph S. Alemany, Santa Barbara, July 22, 1861.

[20]AALA, Thaddeus Amat to Joseph S. Alemany, San Francisco, October 15, 1861.

countable for any future maintenance expenses incurred without his approval. It was at this juncture that Bishop Amat felt compelled to withdraw completely from the administration of the college and to appeal the case to Rome. In the summer of 1862 he informed the archbishop:

> Since you have made up your mind to establish the college of Santa Ines in San Isidro Ranch where I know it cannot go on well without great expense; and placed, as it must be in said locality out of the inspection of the clergymen of Santa Ines; I, therefore, by these presents, make a formal renunciation of the administration of said college, and I will give notice of the same as soon as possible to the present president of the college that he may apply to you for the direction until it shall be transferred.[21]

Amat's decision was deeply disquieting to the Archbishop of San Francisco. As a matter of fact, earlier that year, Alemany had agreed to submit the question to arbitration and names of several impartial churchmen had been suggested, among them the Archbishop of Baltimore and the Archbishop of Oregon City. The two disputants finally settled on the Jesuit rector of Saint Ignatius College in San Francisco, the Reverend Nicolas Congiato. The latter's decision, dated August 12, came after Amat's withdrawal and, therefore, was not binding on either party. Father Congiato stated:

> . . . whereas all the difficulties existing between their Lordships the Archbishop and the Bishops of California, in relation to the Ranch and College of Santa Ines, have been referred to Rome for final decision, the Right Rev. Bishop of Monterey has no right to demand at present of the Most Rev. Archbishop of San Francisco the payment of his *pro-rata of* the expenses made by the aforesaid Right Reverend Bishop of Monterey for repairing certain buildings used as a college.[22]

[21]AALA, Thaddeus Amat to Joseph S. Alemany, Santa Ines, July 12, 1862.
[22]AALA, Decision of Arbitrator, San Francisco, August 12, 1862.

The decision reflected Amat's appeal which had not yet been acted upon at Rome. Word from Alessandro Barnabo, Cardinal Prefect of Propaganda, was delayed until March 21, 1863, when Alemany informed his suffragan of the tentative official Roman decision, which stated that "the administration be confided to the Bishop of Monterey or to another person, if it will be more pleasing, to be chosen in accordance with the above mentioned Bishop and with the Vicar of Lower California, and let the income be divided *pro-rata* of the co-ownership according to the form of the decision of the same congregation."[23] The ruling was happily received by Bishop Amat as was indicated when he told the archbishop:

> I consider the decision of His Eminence . . . as an act of justice to me, having been forced, merely for the sake of peace, to abandon the administration of the College Ranch which gave occasion to some inhabitants of this place to suspect my honesty in said administration.[24]

Rome's final judgment was received on August 3,[25] and advised against selling the ranch until a more thorough investigation could be made concerning the value of the land. The decision of Propaganda was capable of several interpretations, although it would seem to have been a decided victory for Bishop Amat in that the original *status quo* was to be continued indefinitely. In the meantime Father Croke had given over the administration of the college to a group of Franciscan Third Order Brothers who had come to California from New York against the advice of the Right Reverend John Loughlin, Bishop of

---

[23]AALA, Joseph S. Alemany to Thaddeus Amat, San Francisco, June 2, 1863.

[24]AALA, Thaddeus Amat to Joseph S. Alemany, San Luis Obispo, June 26, 1863.

[25]*"Pro nunc non expedire et interim exquirendas informationes super valore fundi et an commodari divisionem admittat."* AALA, Joseph S. Alemany to Thaddeus Amat, San Francisco, October 9, 1862.

Brooklyn.[26] The Brothers had been temporarily sheltered at Santa Barbara Mission by the generous Father Rubio who, at the time, was unaware of their recent trouble in the east. Croke had also consented to the moving of the college "from the Mission buildings to the old house near the river."[27] The litigation in this case remained unsolved during Bishop Amat's lifetime and it lingered for some years after his death. That both bishops had been anxious for a solution was, of course, true and one can see it reflected in Amat's words when he told the archbishop:

> As to the management of the College for the future, which I renounced, only to be freed from the difficulties you had raised, and which have been settled by the Holy See, I have no difficulty to leave it in your hands, I am sure it will be well attended. . . .[28]

The college continued to function at San Isidro although it never really prospered.

Meanwhile, in 1853, Archbishop Alemany opened a small seminary at Mission Dolores in San Francisco and thereafter he had no need to look to the college for vocations for his archdiocese. When the Franciscan Brothers withdrew in 1877, Alemany, still acting as the administrator of this "extra territorial" holding, handed over the institution to the Christian Brothers who governed it until it was closed in 1882. But for some years previous to this, most of the students had been from San Francisco and Bishop Amat had little if any contact with the institution. The Franciscan chronicler summarized the rather colorful history of the college in this way:

[26]Zephryin Engelhardt, O.F.M., *Mission Santa Ines* (Santa Barbara, 1932), p. 102.

[27]AALA, James Croke to Racca, n.p., October 16, 1862.

[28]AALA, Thaddeus Amat to Joseph S. Alemany, Los Angeles, October 21, 1862.

. . . the 33 years of the College's existence was a transition period between the glorious days of old when saintly and industrious friars reaped a rich harvest of souls and the modern far-flung province that has passed its Second Spring.[29]

SAINT VINCENT'S COLLEGE

From his earliest days in California, Bishop Amat had envisioned a seminary staffed by his own community, and the difficulties he experienced with Santa Ines College served to increase the bishop's hopes in that direction. However, the recent expansion of the Vincentians' American province into Mexico had greatly dispersed its already meager membership and the bishop was compelled to put off his Seminary plan for many years. But if it was not feasible for the Vincentians to undertake the operation of a seminary they were to be identified with religious education in the diocese in other ways as the years progressed. Soon after his appointment to Los Angeles in 1856, Father Blasius Raho, C.M. re-opened the school for boys established by the Picpus Fathers in 1851, despite the fact that the city council had voted to withdraw all subsidies to private schools.[30] The institution was moderately successful and was known as Saint Vincent's College,[31] a title not to be identified with the later establishment[32] bearing that name.

In the spring of 1861, Amat had sent four students to Saint Vincent's College at Cape Girardeau, Missouri, for seminary training. The college had suffered a loss in enrollment during the troubled times of the Civil War and was

[29]*Provincial Annals* (Santa Barbara Province, California), II (October, 1948). p. 53.

[30]Harris Newmark, *op. cit.,* p. 105.

[31]Amat's account statements may be found in North, *op. cit.,* p. 115.

[32]William A. Spalding, *History and Reminiscences of Los Angeles City and County, California* (Los Angeles, n.d.), p. 135.

desirous of increasing its student body by enlisting boys from the entire country. With this in mind, the Vincentian provincial, Stephen V. Ryan, C.M. sent out letters to a number of bishops. His report[33] mentioned that there were then only twenty-nine seminarians, eighteen having been raised to the dignity of the priesthood in addition to what was described as the "four prepared and sent for ordination to the Right Reverend Bishop of Monterey." Ryan's letter provided Amat with an ideal opportunity for opening negotiations about the Vincentians establishing a college or seminary in the Diocese of Monterey-Los Angeles. The bishop made known his wishes to Father Ryan[34] in the spring of 1863 and the latter's reply was optimistic:

> . . . after much reflection and consideration, I think it may be the will of God that we send to your distant mission two or three confreres, who may be able to commence an establishment of this Congregation there and attend to the spiritual needs of the Sisters. . . .[35]

Ordinarily Amat made his visitations in the northern part of his diocese in the summer and this, no doubt, was the reason for his delay in answering Ryan's letter. In answer to his letter in October, he received the following reply:

> I was long awaiting your reply and, seeing that it did not come, I gave a temporary mission to two of the confreres intended for you, and the third, Mr. Burlando, manifested so great a reluctance to go such a distance that the Superior General is unwilling to press him, so that we will have to look around for a suitable person to fill his place . . . and hence we will not be able to send you the confreres until next spring.[36]

[33] AALA, Stephen Ryan to Thaddeus Amat, Cape Girardeau, December 15, 1862.
[34] Ryan afterward became Bishop of Buffalo and was consecrated on November 3, 1863.
[35] AALA, Stephen Ryan to Thaddeus Amat, Saint Louis, July 10, 1863.
[36] AALA, Stephen Ryan to Thaddeus Amat, Saint Louis, November 18, 1863.

But in late December, Father Ryan made it known that, contrary to expectations, he would be able to send "the long promised colony to found a house of the Congregation and take the direction of the good Sisters."[37] Ryan instructed Father John Asmuth then at Baltimore to obtain information from the Sisters of Charity and to proceed, with Father John Beakey, to Los Angeles. The third member of the party, Father J. Pyggott, was then very ill and in the end was replaced by Father Michael Rubi. Asmuth was designated superior. The priests reached Los Angeles in March of 1864[38] where they found the place sorely afflicted by an extreme and disastrous drought, a fact which undoubtedly influenced the tone of their reports to Father Ryan. In addition there arose a difficulty regarding the terms upon which Bishop Amat proposed to establish their new foundation. Father Asmuth's instructions, at least as he understood them, were to accept the foundation only if the title to the property was vested absolutely in the Congregation of the Mission. The bishop, on the other hand, quoted the diocesan statutes to the contrary and cited two letters from Cardinal Barnabo to the same effect. The negotiations became deadlocked since Asmuth felt himself unable to meet the bishop's terms and accordingly, the fathers left Los Angeles and Father Asmuth passed on to his provincial the news of this development.

In May of the same year, the three Vincentians were in San Francisco where they again met Amat who was there on business. On this occasion he offered them perpetual use of the diocesan acreage in Pajaro Valley near Watsonville, but again he was unsuccessful in altering their views. The matter remained in abeyance until August dur-

[37]AALA, Stephen Ryan to Thaddeus Amat, Saint Louis, December 30, 1863.

[38]Father Asmuth suffered a violent hemorrhage on the voyage from Panama to San Francisco and arrived in a very feeble condition.

ing which time the Vincentians entered upon negotiations with Bishop Eugene O'Connell of Grass Valley for a settlement in the latter's diocese. Meanwhile the fathers occupied their time giving missions in the prosperous mining camps of Nevada and on August 4, Father Asmuth, with the provincial's approval, notified Amat of their intention of locating in the Diocese of Grass Valley.

Meanwhile Amat had sent his views of the case to Father Ryan, but his letter did not reach the provincial until midway through the summer. Ryan replied that he had no knowledge of either the special statutes of the diocese or of the views of Propaganda regarding the tenure of property. He mentioned, however, that he did not regard this development as an insuperable obstacle. He said:

> But the location and prospects of success and future usefulness at the different points in Your Lordship's diocese, visited and examined by those personally and deeply interested, were far from encouraging. Hence I have written to our good confreres to settle themselves in any eligible position in San Francisco or any neighboring diocese, wheresoever they may find the greatest facilities to carry out the works of the Community, to establish a little Seminary or a house for missions, retreats, etc. and to attend to the direction of the Sisters of Charity. A central and quickly populated locality with facilities of communication and of easy access is certainly preferable to a remote and sparsely settled country.[39]

In his lengthy reply Amat reiterated his position in the matter of the property and expressed his regret that the congregation could not accept his offer for the direction of a *petit seminaire* in Los Angeles. In enlarging upon the advantages of Pajaro as a site for the seminary, he said:

> Any other community, knowing the place, would immediately accept it; the Jesuits would hasten to it with satisfaction, as

[39]AALA, Stephen Ryan to Thaddeus Amat, Saint Louis, August 8, 1864.

they have also offered to accept the place which I proposed
to our confreres here in Los Angeles, which cannot fail, although poor today as there is no town or city in California so
much favored with water for irrigation, the principal element
wanted in California.[40]

Pajaro, the bishop thought, would soon be connected with
San Francisco by rail. He also offered the fathers a parish
in nearby Watsonville where a church was already under
construction, until such a time as they might be able to
finance themselves in their own house. The region, settled
mainly by Irish Catholics, was one of rich land, easily ir-
rigated. He remained optimistic that the Vincentians
would ultimately accept his offer either of Pajaro or Los
Angeles. This last letter seems to have reopened the whole
question, for on December 3, Ryan wrote again, saying
that he had communicated with Father Asmuth with the
result that "if anything should turn up to prevent their establishment where they now propose to settle, I think he
might very well accept Pajaro Valley, provided they have
a guaranty of a secure and permanent house."[41]

The upshot of all this was the return, in the spring of
1865, of the Vincentians to Los Angeles. Without relin-
quishing his idea of a minor seminary he went along with
their plans to open a school for boys and an announcement
was duly made to this effect. In April, Amat called together a group of representative men to discuss plans for
establishing a college, and on May 2, a ways-and-means
committee was suggested and approved. Support came
from outside the Catholic community and as one local historian has said:

Soon afterward, the ladies of the community, at a fair suggested and guided by Mrs. Rose Newmark, an incident pleas-

[40]AALA, Thaddeus Amat to Stephen Ryan, n.p., October 13, 1864.
[41]AALA, Stephen Ryan to Thaddeus Amat, Cape Girardeau, December 3, 1864.

antly reminding one of the charming tolerance then existing among Los Angeles citizens, secured several hundred dollars for the desired educational fund.[42]

A formal agreement between the Vincentian Fathers and Bishop Amat with reference to educational work in the diocese was signed on May 9, 1865.[43] The bishop reserved the right to place his seminarians in the college—which it was said, was being established "under the tutelage of the priests of the Congregation of the Mission, according to their rules." And, if in the future, it should seem advisable to introduce lay students, the seminary part of the enterprise could be handed over to different instructors.[44] The fathers were also given permission on June 13, to collect funds throughout the diocese to erect and support the college. Amat noted that by virtue of an oral agreement with Father Asmuth, the Vincentians would not open their chapel for public use, lest the parish church be affected. With regard to this latter point, the bishop left himself free to act in the future as seemed best to him. Under the caption "Collegiate Action" the Los Angeles correspondent of the *Alta California* wrote:

> The citizens of this place have been awakened to the necessity as well as the benefits that will flow from the founding of a college in the southern part of California. Meetings have been held . . . to cooperate with the Bishop . . . in securing the aid necessary to carry out the idea. The evenness of the temperature of this place . . . will be appreciated by students and their guardians.[45]

[42]Harris Newmark, *op. cit.*, p. 112.

[43]AALA, Documents signed May 9, 1865 at Los Angeles.

[44]There was no seminary formally established in Los Angeles until 1927 when Los Angeles College opened under the guidance of the Vincentian Fathers. In 1939 the Congregation of the Mission took charge of Saint John's Seminary at Camarillo, California. In addition to their own minor seminary in Montebello, the Vincentians also staff the new senior seminary of the archdiocese at Camarillo, opened in 1961.

[45]June 13, 1865 (under date of June 4).

And on August 5 the following advertisement appeared in the local paper:

ST. VINCENT SELECT SCHOOL FOR BOYS

At the request of the Right Rev. Bishop, the Priests of the Congregation of the Mission are about to open a Select School in Los Angeles, for the educatoin of the boys of this city and the surrounding country. They contemplate building a College as soon as the necessary funds shall be obtained. For the present they have rented LUGO HOUSE ON THE PLAZA. School will be opened in this house on or about the 17th day of August.[46]

The college got under way in early September in the rented adobe house of Don Vicente Lugo with Father Asmuth as superior and president. The existence of the college was, indeed precarious, for it was soon jeopardized by a lack of funds as well as by deaths on its faculty. Within a year both Father Asmuth and Father Beakey died and the Vincentians were on the verge of closing the college when in 1866 the munificence of Mr. O. W. Childs[47] provided a tract of nine acres[48] south of Sixth Street running almost to Eighth. Father James McGill, the president, immediately drew up plans for a new college building which he envisioned for the northwest corner of the property, that is, at Sixth and Hill Streets. A handsome two-story brick structure was quickly erected with, as it was said, "contributions from the county and city and from prominent citizens. . . ."[49] Faculty and students moved into their new quarters early in March and on Sunday, March 17, 1867, the new college was dedicated by Father Rubi, in the absence of Bishop Amat who was in Wash-

---

[46]Los Angeles *News*, August 5, 1865.

[47]AALA, James McGill to Thaddeus Amat, Los Angeles, June 19, 1866.

[48]William A. Spalding, *op. cit.*, p. 171.

[49]Josephine Hessel, "The History of the Catholic Church in Los Angeles," (Los Angeles, 1937), p. 30.

ington on diocesan business. A solemn Mass was celebrated and a sermon on the value of a good education was preached by Father Rubi. According to one account, "a large concourse of citizens from the city and county assembled to witness the ceremonies,"[50] a fact which must have gratified the fathers who would perhaps, see here the effect of their influence in the city. The following week's paper dedicated an editorial to the college where, it was said, the city's "sons can be elegantly educated whilst their physical energies are being fully developed."

> . . . We feel no hesitation in saying that nowhere on the Pacific coast, will parents or guardians find a more desirable institution in every requisite particular for the education of those under their charge than the one to which we refer. The gentlemen who are in charge of the College of Saint Vincent are well known to us, and we assert that no more accomplished scholars and gentlemen can be found in any institution in or out of the State of California.[51]

A charter from the State of California was granted to the college on August 15, 1869, empowering it to confer certain degrees and to function as a university. Soon thereafter, Amat proudly communicated this happy news to Archbishop Alemany:

> We have much pleasure in being able to state, that this institution has obtained its charter, in accordance with the proceedings which we published some time ago, and that Saint Vincent's is now duly authorized to confer degrees for scholarship, issue diplomas, and to do all and everything pertaining to a college of first class standing. . . .[52]

The college continued to prosper in subsequent years and proved to be one of the most stabilizing features of Catho-

[50]Los Angeles Daily *News,* March 19, 1867.

[51]*Ibid.,* April 2, 1867.

[52]AALA, Thaddeus Amat to Joseph S. Alemany, n.p., n.d.

lic life in Los Angeles. Its graduates still serve the state and one of its more notable sons recently completed two terms as Governor of California. During a visit to Los Angeles in 1876, the Archduke Ludwig Salvador left a quaint description of the college when he said:

> The Catholic College of Saint Vincents is situated in the west end of town in a pleasant garden. It is a large, ugly building, with seven windows and a gable, in front surmounted by a cross and ball. Through the building runs a central corridor. On the second floor are the dormitories. The College also contains a library and a small chapel. From the terrace, an excellent view may be had over the city of Los Angeles. Out in the garden is a vine covered pergola where the boys gather. In front of the house stands a small fountain. This institution has three classes with the enrollment last year of some seventy students. Of course, the majority are Catholics.[53]

Amat's personal dedication to the cause of a sound and balanced Catholic education and its necessity in his diocese are evident in all his actions and more concretely in his own written words:

> In an affair of so great importance, Catholic parents are to be seriously admonished daily more and more to watch over their children and diligently see and assiduously labor to secure for them a thorough Catholic education. Let them . . . generously offer their goods that Catholic and parochial schools may, with the least possible delay, be erected and supported.[54]

The bishop's zeal in promoting education within the diocese spoke for itself. When he arrived in the see in 1855, there was but one struggling college; when he died in 1878, there were two colleges, six academies, nine parochial schools and five orphanages,[55] an impressive total for a diocese that boasted of barely 34,000 Catholic people.

[53]Ludwig Salvador, *Los Angeles in the Sunny Seventies* (Los Angeles, 1929), p. 130.
[54]Thaddeus Amat, C.M., *Pastoral Letter* (Los Angeles, 1869), p. 18.
[55]*Sadlier's Catholic Directory for 1878* (New York, 1878), p. 312.

CHAPTER EIGHT

SAINT VIBIANA AND HER CATHEDRAL

I T WAS early in 1851 that Pope Pius IX purchased a vineyard on the outskirts of Rome bounded by the Via Appia Antica, Via Ardeatina, and Vicolo delle Sette Chiese, directly above a vast series of unexplored catacombs which had gone unknown and unused for almost a thousand years.[1] The first nucleus of this cemetery of Saint Callistus dates to the first half of the 2nd century and was situated, according to one authority, in a piece of ground belonging to the noble family of the Cecili. From this nucleus developed the great necropolis that is one of the largest among the excavated edifices of subterranean Rome. The excavation of the area was entrusted by the Holy Father to the Pontifical Commission for Sacred Archaeology which at that time was under the direction of the famous Giovanni Battista de Rossi.[2] During the month of December, 1853, an examination was made of that portion then known as San Sisto, later commonly referred to by the name of *Pretestato* because of a picture of that saint visible therein. This cemetery was located to the left of the Appian Way

[1]Giovanni Battista de Rossi, *Roma Sotterranea* (Rome, 1882), I, 306.

[2]Giovanni Battista de Rossi (1822-1894) was the founder of the modern science of archaeology.

in a locality about one mile from the Porta di San Sebastino.

Excavations resulted in the discovery of an ancient entrance to the cemetery, one time well cared for, but now in almost complete ruin. On December 9,[3] workmen found a vault containing a number of vials of spices and quite a few marble tablets with epitaphs still remaining intact. Among the sepulchres remaining unbroken was that of a certain Vibiana. To the left and adjoining her tomb was a crystal vase of a red-rose color containing aromatic spices of the newly discovered martyr. A marble stone, seventy centimeters long and thirty wide, with an inscription attached, sealed the sepulchre. The tablet was intact although cracked in several places. When the workmen attempted to remove the tablet, the arch of the tomb, already weakened by the excavations, collapsed and partially buried the tomb. After the debris was removed, the skeleton of a young woman, obviously put to death in a violent fashion, became visible.

The exact date of her death, as well as further information about her person, is uncertain. But from the inscriptions and other epitaphs in the area, it has been conjectured by archaeologists that Vibiana lived in the third century. The inscription on her tomb reads: *Animae innocenti adque pudicae Vibianae in pace D. Pr. K St.* ("To the soul of the innocent and pure Vibiana, laid away the day before the Kalends of September"). At the end of the inscription is a garland of palm leaves, an emblem commonly used by early Christians to symbolize martyrdom and the glorious triumph which martyrs attain. After a personal visit to the catacombs by Pius IX, an investigation

[3]AALA, Statement of Antonio Ferrua, S.J., Secretary of the Pontifical Commission for Sacred Archaeology, Rome, March 11, 1953.

was ordered to ascertain the authentic character of the relics. In February of 1854, they were exposed for public veneration and were known as "the precious relics of the illustrious and glorious Martyr, Vibiana."[4]

Public enthusiasm for the newly discovered relics was manifested not only in the Eternal City itself, but also in the surrounding area and a number of prominent ecclesiastics petitioned Pope Pius for the saint's relics, all without success. It remained for the recently consecrated Bishop of Monterey, Thaddeus Amat, to win the privilege almost without asking.[5] When Amat was received by the Holy Father on March 18, 1854, the generous-minded pontiff conferred the relics on Monterey's new ordinary[6] "with the express condition of building the Cathedral Church in honor of the Saint."[7]

The authentic, granted by the Holy Father's Vicar General, noted that the Pope was giving to:

> The Most Illustrious Bishop of Monterey, Thaddeus Amat, the body of the maiden, Saint Vibiana, unearthed by mandate of Pius IX on December 9, 1853, from the Cemetery of Pretestato (San Sisto) along with a vial of her blood and also a marble slab bearing the inscription 'to the soul of the innocent and pure Vibiana, laid away the day before the Kalends of September.' We hereby affix to the wooden container our engraved testimonial, a chaplet of red colored silk to which is attached our seal.[8]

[4]*Novena a Santa Vibiana, Virgen y Martir, Protectora de la Diocesis de Monterey,* (San Francisco, 1856), p. 4.

[5]This according to a statement by Joseph Mesmer in the *Tidings,* September 4, 1931.

[6]Thaddeus Amat, C.M., *Asociacion de Santa Vibiana, Virgen y Martir,* (Barcelona, 1860), p. 1.

[7]AALA, Rescript of June 1, 1854. *"Cum Reverendissimus Thaddeus Amat, Episcopus Montereyensis, dono exceperit mortales exuvias Stae, Vibianae, Virginis et Martyris, cujus in honorem Deo servandum constituit novam Cathedralem ibi erigendam. . . ."*

[8]AALA, Constantinus, Bishop of Albanensis to Thaddeus Amat, Rome, May 10, 1854.

Bishop Amat brought the relics with him on his journey to California where he arrived in November of 1855. After a short stay in San Francisco, he set out for Monterey and then continued on to Santa Barbara where he disembarked on December 2. On the following Tuesday, feast of Santa Barbara, the relics in an artistically prepared case with a golden crown were borne in solemn procession to the Church of Our Lady of Sorrows[9] in the city where a special shrine was built soon thereafter, to the right of the main altar. It was at this place of devotion that the Catholics of the area came to pay reverence to their new saint. In the following year, on March 28, 1856, Pius IX granted to the Diocese of Monterey a special feastday for Saint Vibiana, an action which was formalized by papal decree of September 1,[10] at which time Saint Vibiana was declared the principal patroness of the diocese. It was also with pontifical authority, that Bishop Amat founded the Association of Saint Vibiana, in 1858. Pius IX prefaced his remarks on the new society with these words:

> Since a pious society of the faithful of both sexes has been canonically erected in the Diocese of Monterey, under the title of Saint Vibiana, patroness of the diocese, and will be attached to the church where Our venerable brother, the present Bishop of Monterey, has informed Us will be built in honor of this saint and martyr, We grant the following indulgences in order that this society may grow in influence and numbers.[11]

The Supreme Pontiff then enumerated the privileges of the society and concluded with the establishment of a privileged altar "at the place where the body of the sacred body of Saint Vibiana is deposited."[12]

[9]Santa Barbara *Gazette,* December 6, 1855.
[10]AALA, Rescript of September 1, 1856.
[11]AALA, Pius IX to Thaddeus Amat, Rome, January 7, 1859, Quoted in *Asociacion de Santa Vibiana, Virgen y Martir,* p. 6.
[12]*Ibid.,* p. 8.

Amat had several aims in mind when he set up the society among which were these:

(1) The primary and principal purpose of the Association was to be the raising of funds to help defray the building costs of a shrine to honor the new patroness;

(2) The enrollment of all members of the society in memorial books to be kept by the senior priests of each parish;

(3) Monthly Mass, celebrated at the shrine for all the benefactors who names were registered in the memorial books.[13]

Further papal interest and approval came on August 17, 1862,[14] after the clergy had requested a transfer of Saint Vibiana's solemnity to the Sunday following her feast day. In December of that year the priests of the diocese were given a proper office for September 1 which carried the rank of second class.

On the afternoon of August 23, 1865, the Church of Our Lady of Sorrows was totally destroyed by fire. The tiny chapel in which the relics of Saint Vibiana rested was also consumed, but the body of the saint, reposing in a glass and metal case, escaped unharmed. Although the reliquary was badly singed and the glass broken, nothing inside the case was damaged. This seemingly miraculous event created wide commotion and did much to increase popular devotion to the diocesan patroness. When the church was rebuilt, no provisions were made for a new shrine. So Bishop Amat had the relics moved to Los Angeles where they were enshrined in the Church of Our Lady of the Angels.

Devotion to Saint Vibiana has continued through the years even to the present day. At the time of the golden jubilee of Saint Vibiana's Cathedral in 1926, the diocesan

[13]*Ibid.,* p. 2.

[14]AALA, Rescript of August 17, 1862.

newspaper, in an editorial addressed to the Catholics of Los Angeles, had this to say about the saint:

> The body of the Saint who is the patroness of the Cathedral and the diocese was given to this far-distant part of the Lord's vineyard in the days before the church was built. It was reverently brought to these shores from its resting place in the darkness of the Roman catacombs to be enshrined at last, here in our midst, with becoming pomp and ceremony. There, in the niche high above the main altar of the Cathedral her relics have rested in peace for half a century, while from her heavenly home this gentle maiden has watched over the destinies of a now great diocese and lent a ready ear to those who have sought her intercession. It is much to be regretted that we have not developed a stronger devotion to the sainted patroness of our diocese and its principal church. We can have no doubt that she will be anxious to intercede for us, her spiritual children, in a very special manner.[15]

THE ERECTION OF THE CATHEDRAL

As early as 1856, reports began appearing in local newspapers about a proposed cathedral. The Santa Barbara *Gazette* stated on May 22 of that year that "it is the intention of Bishop Amat to commence soon the erection of a cathedral in Santa Barbara, near the site of the present chapel. . . ."[16] In any case, whatever plans there might have been were postponed until the Holy See handed down its decision transferring the seat of the diocese to Los Angeles in 1859.

When Amat came back from Europe in January of 1868, he turned his attention to the long cherished project for which he had been setting aside funds for several years. Los Angeles was beginning its recovery from the protracted drought of 1862 and with a gradual increase in

[15]Charles C. Conroy, *The Centennial* (Los Angeles, 1940), p. 79.
[16]Santa Barbara *Gazette,* May 22, 1856.

agricultural prosperity, it was hoped that a prosperous era would dawn for the region. Amat appointed a committee to promote the project and a property site was acquired on the west side of Main Street, a little north of Sixth, together with an adjacent lot fronting on Spring Street. The new cathedral would be dedicated, by express wish of Pius IX,[17] to Saint Vibiana and would enshrine the maiden's relics which had been brought to Los Angeles from Santa Barbara in 1868 and placed temporarily in a chapel of Our Lady of the Angels Church.

By the end of 1868, the preliminary planning was completed. The following year was a noteworthy one in the annals of California for it saw the transcontinental railway in the north completed in May. Locally, a line was built from Los Angeles to Wilmington and the prospects of a southern roadbed were also promising. All these developments emphasized the need for the Catholic Church to have a fitting cathedral in the expanding city. Sufficient water was available, a bank was in operation and, a smallpox scare notwithstanding, money was fairly plentiful. Speculation in land was rife, and for a short time, reached "boom" proportions. Interest in the proposed cathedral was obvious in all centers. One paper carried the news in terms more fanciful than true:

> The Catholics contemplate building a cathedral at a cost of about forty thousand dollars. Yesterday morning a paper was circulated and about five thousand dollars subscribed in a little time.[18]

The first official announcement of the bishop's plans was read in the churches of the diocese on Sunday, June 6, 1869. After stressing the necessity of better attendance

---

[17]". . . with the express condition of building a cathedral in honor of the Saint."
[18]Los Angeles *Republican,* April 15, 1869.

of children at catechetical instructions, a formal declaration of the building project was made:

> We cannot close these lines without informing you of our initiatory steps toward commencing our Cathedral Church in honor of our Patroness, Saint Vibiana, whose sacred remains we received through the liberality of Our Holy Father, Pius IX, with the express understanding, not to say command, that they should be deposited within its walls. As there is question of the Mother Church of the Diocese to be built in honor of the Patroness of the same, we can entertain no doubt that every one of our faithful children in Christ will hasten with generosity to assist us in bringing it to a speedy and perfect completion.[19]

Bishop Amat had planned to attend the First Vatican Council scheduled to convene in Rome on December 8[20] and it was decided to begin preparatory work on the cathedral before his departure. Cornerstone ceremonies were conducted on October 3, 1869, at four o'clock in the afternoon on property donated by Mr. Ozro W. Childs. Coins, newspapers, and a formal decree, together with other items of historic interest were sealed in a lead box and deposited within the cavity of the Folsom granite stone. A large crowd of people, estimated in excess of 3,000 braved the blistering heat to attend the historic function.[21] A long religious procession moved down Main Street to the music of the United States Military Band from Drum Barracks. First, in carriages, was Bishop Amat accompanied by the priests of the diocese. Then along the sidewalk came the Sisters of Charity with their students and finally in the rear a huge line of the faithful and friends of the Church. When the procession had arrived at the

[19]Quoted in the *Alta California*, June 15, 1869.
[20]AALA, "*Libro Gobierno*," p. 68.
[21]Los Angeles *Star*, October 7, 1869.

proposed site, Pontifical Mass was celebrated. An episcopal blessing was given to the area where the main altar
would be erected.[22] A sermon in English[23] was preached
by Father James McGill, C.M., president of Saint Vincent's
College followed by one in Spanish delivered by the
bishop.

After Amat's departure for Rome, work on the cathedral
lagged and was soon suspended completely. Hard times
had again overtaken the city and the smallpox epidemic,
while not overly serious, frightened investors away. The
hope of silk-culture as a leading industry also grew slim.
In short, money became unobtainable and the entire project was discontinued. There was also a rather prevalent
opinion that the cathedral site was too far out of town.
The college with its private chapel was only two blocks
away and although the Vincentians had agreed not to open
their chapel for public use, it seemed extravagant to build
a massive cathedral so close to existing facilities.

Upon Amat's return from Europe, a new site was selected further north yet considerably south of the plaza.
Amat had acquired property in that area in August of
1858 from Amiel Cavallier.[24] It was an attractive piece of
land with a small stream flowing through the middle. The
bishop petitioned the city for a deed of quitclaim and received assurance that such a request would be granted.[25]
In May, 1871, Amat gave his formal approval and the
work of clearing the ground began. The enterprise, like
all others of the time, was closely linked to the ups and
downs of agricultural and sheep raising interests. The win-

[22]Los Angeles Daily *News,* October 5, 1869.

[23]Quoted *verbatim* in the Los Angeles *Star,* October 7, 1869.

[24]Deed Book, Book IV, p. 204.

[25]The quitclaim granted by the City of Los Angeles to Thaddeus Amat was
dated December 14, 1877.

ters of 1868-1870 were exceptionally dry and, therefore, economically unfavorable. Hence, in order to adjust the original plans along more modest lines, a smaller church was designed by the local architect, E. F. Kyser, who in later days was assisted by W. J. Mathews with whom he formed a partnership. The general plan of the structure was suggested by that of the Iglesia de Puerto de San Miguel in Barcelona[26] and provided for a building eighty feet wide and 160 feet deep.

Beyond the clearing of the property, little work was done in 1871. The outer walls took form in 1872 and 1873 in a seemingly endless succession of delays. Bishop Amat went to Europe for his health in 1874 and during his absence his coadjutor, Bishop Francis Mora, renewed efforts to complete the structure before Amat's return. Louis Mesmer took charge of the construction program in the winter of 1874-1875 and "inaugurated a renewal of the work by bringing to it an energy which never flagged until the structure was ready for divine services."[27]

By the end of June, 1875, the building had been roofed. The giant bell of Mission San Juan Capistrano, cast in Massachusetts in 1828, was blessed on July 4 and on the following day a festival was held to raise funds for the continuance of the work. A group of ladies sponsored the gala affair within the bare brick walls[28] and it was estimated "that at least three thousand visitors were present during the day and partook of the elegant bounty."[29] On Sunday afternoon, January 2, 1876, the foundation stone of the

[26]The Puerto de San Miguel was damaged by a severe earthquake toward the close of the last century; hence a great deal of renovation on the historic church was necessary. Today there is a notable discrepancy in the stateliness of the exterior from the magnificent proportions of the interior.

[27]Los Angeles *Express,* April 10, 1875.

[28]*Ibid.,* July 4, 1875.

[29]*Ibid.,* July 6, 1875.

high altar was blessed and set in place.[30] Later additions
were no less newsworthy:

> The cupola of the new Church is, without exception, the most
> graceful specimen of architecture in California. It is a marvel
> of symmetrical beauty and comely shapeliness. The eye just
> naturally lingers on it, and never tires of admiring its elegance
> and handsome proportions. That beautiful tower will yet be
> sung in verse and commemorated in lasting prose.[31]

In the first months of 1876, the work of decorating the
interior and exterior of the church was undertaken by
Joaquin Amat, the bishop's nephew. The artistic stone-
work for the railing in front of the building was manu-
factured in blocks in East Los Angeles at the artificial stone
factory of Messrs. Bashard and Hamilton. Railings, fabri-
cated from iron, products of Page and Gravel, formed a
beautiful and suitable enclosure which lasted for many
years. The two niches flanking the rose window received
statues of SS. Peter and Paul, and on the upper front wall
of the transepts images of the four evangelists were attached. Statues of SS. Patrick and Emigdius were placed
at either side of the main altar.[32] At last, on Palm Sunday,
April 9, the first services were held within the cathedral
walls. The palms were blessed at ten o'clock after which
a solemn pontifical Mass was celebrated in the presence of
the city's leading dignitaries. The spacious new church
easily accommodated the immense throng gathered for
the joyous occasion. Immediately after the Mass, Bishop
Amat imparted a special apostolic blessing and offered a
few words of gratitude to his flock.

The colorful ceremonies of consecration were scheduled
for the second Sunday after Easter, April 30. Archbishop

[30]*Ibid.*, December 31, 1875.
[31]*Ibid.*, February 11, 1876.
[32]*Ibid.*, April 8, 1876.

Alemany of San Francisco officiated and celebrated the Mass. The renowned Indian Jesuit priest, Father James Bouchard, gave an historical description of the symbolic ceremonies of which the only extant report says the

> . . . eloquent divine gave a graphic description of the cere-
> monies of consecration, and illustrated in a lucid manner all
> the symbols and mysteries of the magnificent spectacle. He
> spoke of the building of the Temple of Solomon, and com-
> pared the work of erecting a modern Tabernacle of God; he
> made a fervent appeal on behalf of religion and religious
> works, and adjured his hearers to turn from the sinful ways
> of the world and consecrate their souls to God.[33]

At the conclusion of the consecration rite, Bishop Amat was host to the archbishop and various civic officials at a banquet in the episcopal residence. Alemany delivered an interesting address outlining the historical background of the California apostolate, recalling the somewhat-forgotten trials and tribulations that plagued the early missionaries. To these pioneers, Alemany gave the credit for planting the seed that blossomed forth into Saint Vibiana's Cathedral.

A solemn procession was scheduled for six o'clock[34] to translate the relics of Saint Vibiana from the Plaza to her permanent shrine above the cathedral's main altar. Headed by the Mexican brass band, several of the city's societies, followed by more than 200 children, formed the honor guard. Father John Basso carried the metropolitan cross followed by sixteen priests chanting the litany of the saints. The shrine itself was borne by four priests, vested in alb and stole. Archbishop Alemany and Bishop Mora came behind the shrine and the aging Bishop Amat, ex-

[33]Quoted in John B. McGloin, S.J., *Eloquent Indian* (Berkeley, 1950), p. 292.
[34]Thomas Atwill Neal, *Saint Vibiana's Los Angeles Cathedral, 1876-1950.* (Los Angeles, 1950), p. 8.

hausted by the long and tiring ceremonials, rode in his carriage. As soon as the procession reached the cathedral, the relics were deposited in the middle of the sanctuary and "a most eloquent and impressive sermon in Spanish was delivered by Archbishop Alemany." At the end of the archbishop's remarks, the clergy sang the *Te Deum* after which Father Joachim Adam delivered a short talk in English. The ceremony was ended with Benediction of the Blessed Sacrament. Early next morning, the crystal and gilt casket containing the relics of Saint Vibiana was raised to its place in a niche above the high altar, in the tower, where it remains to the present day.

CHAPTER NINE

AMAT AT THE FIRST VATICAN COUNCIL

ON December 6, 1864, just two days before the publication of his famous Encyclical, *Quanta Cura,* containing the "Syllabus of Errors," Pope Pius IX announced to the curial cardinals plans for the convocation of an ecumenical council to be held at Rome and subsequently to be known as the First Vatican Council. During the next four years, details and schemata were prepared for discussion by five separate commissions, each charged with a different aspect of the agenda. In a public consistory held on June 26, 1868, the Supreme Pontiff made the public announcement. The official convocation or papal summons, *Aeterni Patris,* was promulgated on June 29 of the following year, and December 8, 1869 was appointed as the date of the formal opening.

The prospect of attending an ecumenical council must have been a fascinating one for the American bishops. When the last council sat at Trent, America had barely been discovered and only a few adventurous priests had arrived to spread the faith among the unknown peoples of the new world. Now that area was to be represented by more than one hundred members of the hierarchy!

Bishop Thaddeus Amat left for Rome on October 7, 1869, proceeding first to San Francisco where he and Archbishop Alemany boarded the "Senator" for Panama. They arrived in the Eternal City in ample time for the opening of the great assembly. The Bishop of Monterey-Los Angeles was a respected theologian with valuable experience in gatherings of this nature. His attendance at three of the Baltimore councils gave him an insight into conciliar procedure, and this experience was to prove highly advantageous to him during the deliberations. When the decision was made regarding the precedence to be followed among the Americans, Amat was designated twelfth in the line of bishops from the United States.

A preliminary session, presided over by the Pope himself, had been held on December 2 in the presence of approximately 500 bishops. At this meeting, the officials of the Council were named and the conciliar procedure made known. Five cardinals were appointed to preside over the sessions. It had been decided to use the right transept of the vast basilica of Saint Peter for the asembly and that area was shut off from the remainder of the church. Inside the council chamber, tribunes or daises hung with tapestries were arranged for royal guests and heads of governments who might be asked to sit in on the council's deliberations. A papal throne was set up at the far end of the room, flanked on either side by benches for the princes of the Church. A raised lectern was placed near the altar.

The morning of December 8 was heavy with rain and in all directions grey clouds could be seen hovering over the seven hills. In spite of the inclement weather, 80,000 people crowded into the basilica while other thousands huddled beneath forests of black umbrellas in Saint Peter's Square. It was an impressive sight to behold nearly 700 silver-coped bishops filing down the grand staircase into the church. When the seventy-seven year old Pontiff was carried into the ancient basilica, it marked the beginning of the first assembly of this kind since 1563.

Of more than 1,000 fathers in attendance at one time or another during the ecumenical council, the great majority were politically in the center or on the right. On the extreme right were the ultra-montanes, headed by Henry Edward Manning, Archbishop of Westminster, who it was said, "is more Catholic than Catholics."[1] This group was anxious to strengthen the central authority of the Church by a swift proclamation of papal infallibility. A minority of so-called liberals led by Felix Dupanloup, Bishop of Orleans, was hopeful that the Roman Curia would adapt itself to a more progressive policy in relation to the world around it. A middle position was taken by such prominent ecclesiastics as Archbishop Martin J. Spalding of Baltimore, who desired to see the doctrine defined but without the term "infallibility" which, he claimed, had unfavorable connotations among many non-Catholics, Bishop Amat's position on the delicate question was much the same as Spalding's[2] and was dictated by his ever present concern for the impact such a definition would have in his own diocese where a strong current of non-Catholic feeling existed even at this time.

When, in early January of 1870, the schema drawn up by the famous Jesuit theologian, Giovanni Franzelin, was introduced with its proposed definition of papal infallibility, nearly half the American Bishops declared themselves opposed to the definition, among them Archbishops Peter

[1]William E. Gladstone, *History of the Vatican Council* (New York, 1874), p. 72.

[2]John Lancaster Spalding, *The Life of Most Rev. M. J. Spalding* (Baltimore, 1873), p. 383.

Richard Kenrick of St. Louis and John B. Purcell of Cincinnati. The American bishops were greatly divided though, not only on this matter but on much of the agenda that would confront the council before its conclusion. But in the matter of infallibility, which was clearly the most controversial of the whole council, Kenrick, was "violently opposed to the definition, not only because of what he considered its inopportuneness, but because he did not see it was part of the deposit of faith."[3] Archbishop McCloskey of New York, Archbishop Purcell and twenty other bishops went so far as to sign Kenrick's inopportunist petition to the Holy Father. Their position was decidedly a minority opinion and although they seem to have sensed this early, an effort was made to prevent a decision as long as possible. Such tactics, they hoped, would add to their number of adherents, especially in view of the growing critical attitude reflected in the world's press.[4]

Kenrick's main contention was his belief that the doctrine of papal infallibility was, at most, only a probably certain doctrine, and therefore, not capable of formal definition.[5] He persisted in this view even after a previous query on the definability of the doctrine had been answered in the affirmative by the commission of theologians entrusted with drawing up the agenda. It had been their view, however, that such action ought not to be proposed by the Council of the Apostolic See, unless at the petition of the bishops. Kenrick hoped that by raising sufficient doubt as to the soundness of the doctrine, such a proposal

[3] James Gibbons, A Retrospect of Fifty Years (Baltimore, 1916), I, 32.

[4] Cuthbert Butler, The Vatican Council (London, 1930), I, 207. For an excellent treatment of the attitude of the American press toward the Vatican Council, see J. Ryan Beiser, The Vatican and the American Secular Newspapers, 1869-1870 (Washington, D.C.), 1941.

[5] Jean Dominique Mansi, Sacrorum conciliorum nova et amplissima collectio (Leipzig, 1927), XLIX, 668.

would be made. He went so far as to say that "those numerous and learned Catholic theologians who maintained the infallibility of the Roman Pontiff . . . consider it as a matter of *opinion* more or less certain, not as one of Catholic *faith*. Though *not* an article of Catholic faith, it is, however, the general belief among Catholics."[6]

Amat's view, on the other hand, was based completely on the question of so-called public relations. He believed the doctrine's definition highly inadvisable although certainly part of the deposit of faith. As Cardinal Manning remarked in his memoirs, "The only question was whether it was expedient, prudent, seasonable, and timely, regard being had to the conditions of the world, of the nations of Europe, of the Christians in separation from the Church, to put this truth in the form of a definition."[7] And it was Amat's concern for these conditions that compelled him to join a coalition of twenty-seven prelates of English speaking countries, twenty of them American, in expressing formal disapproval of presenting the doctrine at that time. A petition was drafted and sent to the pope on January 15, 1870 incorporating these views:

> We humbly and sincerely beg that the question of defining the infallibility of the Supreme Pontiff as a dogma of faith will not be proposed to the Council . . . because,
>
> a Discussion of the question will clearly show a lack of unanimity, especially among the bishops;
>
> b This definition, far from making the Church more attractive, might further alienate those whom we desire to win back by prayer and sacrifice to Christ;
>
> c We foresee that unlimited strife will arise from this definition which we fear might impede our ministry and destroy

[6]Peter Richard Kenrick, *An Inside View of the Vatican Council* (New York, 1871), p. 143.

[7]Henry Edward Manning, *The True Story of the Vatican Council* (London, 1877), p. 101.

completely the fruits of this Vatican Council among non-believers.[8]

While these three reasons alleged against the definition were extrinsic and as such did not touch the doctrine itself, the hostile press seized upon the minority petition as though it proceeded from an organized "international opposition" that would wreck the work of the council. The *Alta California* gleefully announced that Bishop Amat's determination to side with this point of view "implies that he belongs to the more liberal class of Catholic prelates,"[9] a statement that was not true if one had in mind the philosophical liberalism of the day! Amat's views were quite similar to those of the Archbishop of Baltimore, who, it was said, "inclined to the opinion that a formal definition would be unnecessary and possibly inexpedient."[10] Bishop Bernard McQuaid of Rochester also opposed infallibility because he thought "there is a determination to pass abstract questions and decrees that may be true enough in themselves, but which will be highly injurious to us in America from the handle they will give our enemies."[11]

Archbishop Joseph Sadoc Alemany of San Francisco held opposite views from those of his suffragan from Monterey-Los Angeles. And in one of the most memorable addresses given at the Council on May 14, 1870, he said that though he did not personally regard the Holy Father as wholly infallible except in those matters which he proposes as supreme pastor and doctor of all the faithful, he did regard definition as imperative. The gentle California

[8]*Acta et decreta conciliorum recentiorum* (Fribourg, 1890), VII, p. 947c.

[9]*Alta California,* May 8, 1870.

[10]Raymond J. Clancy, C.S.C., "American Prelates in the Vatican Council," *Historical Records and Studies,* XXVIII (1937), 40-41.

[11]Frederick J. Zwierlein, "Bishop McQuaid of Rochester," *Catholic Historical Review,* V (January, 1920), 313.

metropolitan added that he spoke out "not to prolong this argument but merely to show that the fear displayed by many about the definition of infallibility is not sufficiently founded."[12] His reasons for appealing to the fathers were based on his contention that "at present this definition is necessary on account of the innumerable errors that daily gain ground and for the reason that once this Council is closed it will be no easy task to assemble another."[13]

Amat was no less vociferous in other matters brought before the Council, and recent studies[14] have given a new prominence to the Bishop of Monterey-Los Angeles and his activities at the historic assembly. Several characteristics are discernible in Amat's action at the council. He was dogmatic, almost picayune in terminology; yet he never hesitated to insist strenuously on the pastoral implication of the legislation. This is nowhere more obvious than in the complete lack of sympathy he had with his own confreres of the Spanish hierarchy who almost unanimously endorsed the infallibility proposal.[15] Nor was Amat given to political maneuvering. He stated his position and let it go at that. He was impervious to pressures from all sides as is evident from his outspoken views.

On March 26, Bishop Amat made his first appearance before the assembly during the discussion of certain phrases in the tract *De Fide Catolica*. He suggested several alterations in the text and advocated a complete revision of two of the canons. Of the eight changes offered by the Bishop of Monterey-Los Angeles, two were adopted, among them a more precise phrasing of man's ability to grasp di-

---

[12]Raymond J. Clancy, *op. cit.*, 41.

[13]Jean Dominique Mansi, *op. cit.*, LII, 42-45. Cf. Butler, *op. cit.*, II, 122.

[14]Umberto Betti, O.F.M., *La Costituzione dommatica "Pastor Aeterns" del Concilio Vaticano*, I (Rome, 1961).

[15]Cuthbert Butler, *op. cit.*, I, 205.

vine revelation without the aid of grace.[16] Chapter II had
declared that divine revelation was necessary for man, not
only because of original sin, but also because Almighty
God deigned that man share in those divine blessings
which entirely prescind from the comprehension of reason.
Amat pointed out that human intelligence is powerless of
itself and cannot comprehend any supernatural truths before revelation and then only to a limited degree. Another
of Amat's recommendations that was accepted by the
fathers, dealt with the delicate point of scriptural interpretation. The decree originally ignored completely the freedom and progress of theological and philosophical science
and learning since Trent, and forbade all interpretation of
Sacred Scripture not in accord with Roman tradition, the
Latin Vulgate, and the unanimous consent of the fathers.
The more liberal fathers argued that the best defense of
the Church was religious science, and that view was sustained when the final draft was made. Amat was also aware
that a new era had dawned for the Church, an era when
ideas and horizons demanded a more progressive policy on
the part of the hierarchy. Nor was he upset at the thought
of incorporating the principle of "progress of dogma" into
the Council's decrees for he saw the theories of Saint Vincent of Lerrins as necessary parts of the overall re-evalua-
tion that was being applied to the Church. Nevertheless,
he was anxious to preserve Tridentine teaching in those
matters where "progress" could be construed as "compromise." In particular he insisted that the teaching
whereby a unanimous opinion of the fathers represented a
reliable indication of scriptural meaning be retained. He
proposed to add to the second phrase an injunction for-
bidding the teaching of any interpretation "contrary to the

[16]Jean Dominique Mansi, *op. cit.,* LI, 146.

unanimous teachings of the Fathers of the Church,"[17] an opinion on which he differed with his metropolitan, Archbishop Alemany of San Francisco.

Another example of Amat's pastoral concern is obvious when, near the end of that session, he asked for and was given the privilege of seconding a motion incorporating previous condemnations handed down by the Council. He advocated, however, that those holding contrary opinions should not be condemned *nominatim* but rather the error itself should be labeled as heretical. The revised constitution was a remarkable defense of the fundamental principles of Christianity against errors of modernism, rationalism, materialism and atheism, and it owed no small point of its clarity of expression to Thaddeus Amat.

The Bishop of Monterey-Los Angeles ascended the ambo again on March 31, requesting permission to address the council. Among other matters offered on this occasion was his recommendation that the Pauline definition of faith conclude the third chapter. Up to that time, only fragmentary statements of the classic Pauline text were discernible. Also, in Chapter III, Amat wanted the word *debere* added at the end of the canon arguing that to omit it would be equivalent to denying that anyone could be brought to the Faith by internal evidence of its credibility. Another example of Amat's thought was his logical observation that the treatise on Faith should follow immediately after the preamble since, as he said, "it seems more fitting first to decide what Faith is and what the authority of the Church teaching is, and then to explain what the Church teaches."[18] When the completed constitution *De Fide Catolica* was submitted for vote on April 12, Bishop Amat registered

[17]*Ibid.*
[18]*Ibid.,* LI, 231-232; 308.

his *placet* or approval.[19] Formal approbation came twelve days later.

Soon after the schema *De Ecclesia Christi* came under discussion, Amat sought a hearing on the chapters setting forth the institution, perpetuity, and nature of the papal primacy. He advocated the inclusion of papal inerrancy in teaching as well as papal primacy in jurisdiction, thus hoping to obviate the need for a separate definition of infallibility. He also submitted the following substitution, which was received without comment, condemning the appeal from papal decrees.

> We condemn the assertions of those who say that assent is not due to the decisions of the Roman Pontiffs in matters of Faith and Morals inasmuch as these decisions are liable to error; or that it is permitted to appeal from such decisions to a future general council as to an authority superior to the Roman Pontiff or what is still more detestable, to appeal then even to secular powers.[20]

Regarding the canons, Amat was the only American to speak. On June 6, he proposed three amendments to the preamble of which the two following were ultimately accepted:

> a) In the second sentence beginning: "Wherefore before He was glorified, etc.," it seems that the words of Holy Scripture, which are quoted, do not retain their real sense and one should rather say: "Wherefore, before He was glorified, He prayed His Father both for the Apostles and for those who through their word would believe in Him, that they all might be one." The rest can be the sequence and it may read: "Just as the Son Himself, and the Father are One, so might they all be one in them."

[19]Five hundred and fifteen voted *placet* and eighty voted *placet juxta modum* (*Ibid.*, LI, 386).

[20]*Ibid.*, LII, 915-920.

b) Section four beginning: "Against which foundation, etc.," should be corrected in the following manner: "And since the gates of hell, bent on the destruction of the Church from her foundation, if such a thing is possible, rise up from all sides with greater fury from day to day against its divinely built foundation, we show, with the Sacred Council approving, that for the protection, safety, and growth of the Catholic flock, it is necessary that the doctrine of the institution, duration, and nature of the Sacred Apostolic primacy, wherein consists the vigor and soundness of the whole Church, be consonant with the ancient and uniform faith of the universal Church, etc.," as in the *Schema*.[21]

Amat gave as his reasons for these suggestions the desire to cling more closely to the meaning of Holy Writ and to the mind of Christ. Summarizing Amat's role in the Council on this point, one historian stated: "In what esteem the Fathers of the Council had, by this time, learned to hold his thought may be gathered from the fact that these amendments were accepted practically verbatim in the final draft of the *Constitutio de Ecclesia Christi*. This is all the more remarkable since no less than seventeen amendments had been introduced and several of the fathers had demanded that the whole deputation be rewritten.

On Tuesday, June 7, Amat prefaced his remarks with a promise of brevity, to which some of the fathers good-naturedly replied, "bene!" He was again the only American to speak, this time concerning the position of Peter in the Church. He thought Peter's position could better be expressed in words other than those before the Council, and on this there were no two opinions among the bishops. A single day sufficed for the discussion.

The position of Peter in the Church should be expressed rather in this way: "Most Blessed Saint Peter, Prince of the Apostles, head and foundation of the Catholic Church, who,

[21]Raymond J. Clancy, *op. cit.*, 57.

by Our Lord Jesus Christ, etc., . . ." It is not traditional to call Saint Peter the prince and head of the apostles and it seems unwise to apply to Saint Peter the title *columna fidei* since the phrase *columna veritatis* is applied, in Holy Scripture, only to the Church.[22]

Another of Amat's suggestions accepted was his wording on papal primacy. In this section, too, the bishop exhibited a thorough knowledge of dogmatic theology gained during his many years as professor in the American missions.

> Instead of saying: "Blessed Peter . . . in his successors, the bishops of the Holy Roman See . . . at all times even down to the present, lives, presides, and exercises judgment so that whoever succeeds to this chair . . . receives the primacy over the universal Church," it would be more forceful to put a period before "so that whoever, etc.," making a new sentence: "Whoever, therefore, legitimately succeeds to this Chair of Peter . . . receives the primacy of the universal Church."[23]

With the expression of the word "legitimately," this last part of Amat's proposal was accepted completely and without debate.

Chapter III of the schema came before the Council two days later and the California bishop advised that the term "pastors of particular churches" was contrary to the liturgical title of bishops which is *pastores ecclesiae*. He also stated that this expression might convey to many the idea that the Church was divided within as were the non-Catholic sects. This further amendment of Amat's was accepted almost verbatim in the final draft.[24]

Amat's reputation among the assembled bishops was growing almost daily. Hence his last minute attempt on June 28 to block the definition of papal infallibility car-

[22]Jean Dominique Mansi, *op. cit.,* LII, 538-539.
[23]*Ibid.*
[24]*Ibid.,* LII, 1275.

ried with it more than a normal amount of interest. Again, his views were close to those of Spalding, who in his famous "compromise" favored the indirect method since it "seems to excel both in force and in simplicity; for it is clearer, and, perhaps, contains more than a formal definition."[25] Amat began his long dogmatic address with a plea for a clearer distinction between primacy of jurisdiction and the primacy of the magisterium, also venturing the opinion that the doctrine of infallibility would be better received if it were couched in less obvious terms. "The definition," he concluded,

> Seems to follow plainly from the text adduced in the schema. . . . This inerrancy ought necessarily to inhere in the primacy of the Roman Pontiff in order to continually preserve unity in the Church. It lays down a doctrine that all the theologians from St. Alphonsus Liguori teach in common.[26]

There was no doubt that Amat was proposing the complete omission of infallibility from the final text,[27] by leaving out the statement that the infallibility of the Roman Pontiff and of the Church have one and the same body of truth for their object. Actually, the entire chapter was later rewritten and the term *magisterium* was added to the title. In its final form, it does not require too close a scrutiny to see the effects of Amat's thought. When the balloting was concluded on July 13, in the last general congregation, Amat's vote was among the sixty-two cast *placet juxta modum* or conditionally favorable, although the majority of the fathers favored the simple and more embracing *placet*. Those voting *placet juxta modum* were required to hand in written reasons for their action. Amat's explanation centered around his criticism of the preamble and cer-

[25]John Lancaster Spalding, *op. cit.*, p. 394.
[26]*Acta et decreta . . . loc. cit.*, p. 755.
[27]Cuthbert Butler, *op. cit.*, II, 103.

tain other minutiae scattered throughout the chapters.[28]

The subject of papal infallibility was of great concern to the Council; without any question it was the most important part of their deliberations. No other issue raised so much controversy as did that one, and no other question produced such a marked line of difference between the bishops and other fathers of the Council.

Amat attended the last solemn session which convened on the overcast, sweltering, muggy morning of July 18, 1870. On that day, 533 fathers gave their assent to the papal definition of infallibility as we know it today. The fathers thus settled the question finally by concluding that such definitions of the Roman Pontiff are irreformable of themselves and not from the consent of the Church. The final draft of the balloting was solemnly carried to the papal throne and presented to the aging but agile Pius IX. On the same day, the Franco-Prussian War broke out and permission was given to the fathers to return to their dioceses with the understanding that they would return to Rome by November 11. On September 8, however, the troops of Victor Emmanuel II entered the Papal States, arriving through the Porta Pia on September 20. The Holy Father was compelled for reasons of practicality to issue the decree *Postquam Dei munere* on October 20, proroguing the council indefinitely. A suggestion of Archbishop Spalding of Baltimore to continue the council at Mechlin in Belgium was never acted on and thus the twentieth ecumenical council never reassembled.

Of the members attending the memorable gathering at the Vatican in 1869-1870, it is safe to say that no American was more respected and few more plain-speaking than the Bishop of Monterey-Los Angeles, a man whose judgment

[28]*Acta et decreta . . . loc. cit.*, p. 1000A.

in theological matters was always sound and well-balanced. In his memoirs of the Council, William B. Ullathorne, Bishop of Birmingham, had this to say about Amat:

> In my estimation, the shrewdest man in the Council, is the young Bishop from California, a native of Spain, but brought up in America, a little man, with broad shoulders and a broad compact head, like that of the first Napoleon. . . . He never speaks above a few minutes, but he hits the nail on the head invariably. He neither argues nor talks but simply proposes amendments on the text and comes down again.[29]

Amat's role in the Vatican Council was one of the most constructive in a life that witnessed many and varied facets of the ministry.

---

[29]Cuthbert Butler, *op. cit.,* II, 113.

CHAPTER TEN

BISHOP OF MONTEREY-LOS ANGELES

THADDEUS AMAT, now officially designated the Bishop of Monterey-Los Angeles, arrived back at Paris in early August of 1859 and from there he wrote several times to Pope Pius IX about the Santa Ines question. While in Paris he paid a number of calls to the headquarters of Propagation de la Foi, elaborating on the needs of the Church in California. From France, Amat journeyed to Ireland where he visited All Hallows College, and left financial drafts for students already destined for the Diocese of Monterey-Los Angeles. With his business apparently finished, Amat prepared to leave for the United States. One secular journal ventured an unusually inaccurate judgement about the success of Amat's European sojourn:

> We hear that Bishop Amat, who has been absent in Europe for sometime past, is on his way home and that he has obtained from the Holy See a subsidy of $85,000 to aid in the construction of a cathedral and a seminary in Los Angeles.[1]

Just before setting out from Ireland, Amat was advised by the Vincentian Superior General to return to Paris where the decision on the Franciscan question was mo-

[1]Sacramento *Bee*, November, 1859.

mentarily expected. Amat changed his plans but when no word had arrived by early spring he decided to visit Spain again in a final effort to enlist priests for his diocese which was still predominantly Spanish-speaking. During his stay in Madrid, he was received by Queen Isabella II whose aid and interest he sought and to whom he explained his hopes of establishing a seminary to supply priests for the dioceses and vicariates of the southwestern United States. After leaving Madrid, Amat went to Barcelona where, through the good offices of the queen, he obtained twelve students, two Italian priests, two Lazarist lay brothers, four Sisters of Charity and two others, a total of twenty-two volunteers for the California apostolate.[2] He then journeyed on to Marseilles and was back in Rome by late June.

By October, Amat had returned once again to Paris where he wrote to his distant relative, Luigi Cardinal Amat, about his plans to leave soon for "my distant mission."[3] In the only extant letter to his distinguished relative, Amat said that God's will was sending him home, unsuccessful in many ways, but happy that the Holy See was fully apprised of his problems.

During Amat's absence from the diocese, Father Blasius Raho, C.M., the vicar general, carried on the affairs of the struggling See and made what progress he could in the face of overwhelming obstacles. The local newspapers were a constant, if not always reliable, mirror of ecclesiastical activities. For example, early in 1860, one writer stated:

> The Catholic Church in this town is enlarging itself. It is to become the future residence of the Bishop, who styles himself "of Monterey and Los Angeles." A site for a new cathedral

[2]AALA, Thaddeus Amat to Berard DeGlageux, Marseilles, June 23, 1860.
[3]AALA, Thaddeus Amat to Luigi Amat, Paris, October 6, 1860.

has been purchased; the buildings to be erected as soon as the funds can be furnished. It was reported that the Pope had appropriated $85,000 for this cathedral, but this is a mistake. No money has been appropriated by Rome. In connection with the cathedral, there is to be erected a House of Probation for the novices of the Sisters of Charity. Padre Raho informs me that the "house" will be erected immediately, that 12 or 15 Sisters from France, are on their way to organize it. . . .[4]

Serious flood damage had occurred to many buildings in Southern California in December, 1859, of which one was the Plaza Church whose northeast corner was undermined by the rising waters and needed immediate attention.[5]

With his return to California, Bishop Amat took up his residence in Los Angeles at Our Lady of the Angels Church, situated on the west side of the city's plaza, the oldest church in the city. By the end of the 1850's native culture was definitely on the decline and the bishop wisely judged that Los Angeles would soon form the hub of activity in the southern part of the state. Hence the move of the diocesan curia to this once sleepy Mexican village was but another indication of Amat's foresight. Nor did Amat's shrewdness go unnoticed among the American hierarchy. His name had become well known by this time, and it was little wonder that the speculation in ecclesiastical circles of both the United States and Europe regarding a suitable candidate for the vacant See of New Orleans was heard even in California. Archbishop Anthony Blanc had died on June 20, 1860, and one of the names frequently mentioned was that of Thaddeus Amat who seemed all the more logical choice because of his familiarity with the area and its customs. Certainly it was more than speculation that prompted the Reverend William G. McCloskey,

---

[4]*Alta California,* January 7, 1860. An article by Mr. Wallace.
[5]Los Angeles *Star,* December 22, 1860.

first rector of North American College, to broach the matter in a note to the Archbishop of Baltimore:

> Father Buteux of Natchez dined with me today and told me that he had been informed that Bishop Amat had been appointed to the vacant See of New Orleans.[6]

But the appointment, if it was ever seriously considered, did not materialize and later that year Pope Pius IX appointed another Vincentian to New Orleans in the person of John Odin, Bishop of Galveston. Amat's influence, nonetheless, was considerable, even in Rome. One of his closest friends, a Belgian priest who had studied with him at Paris, Father Louis Lootens, had been sent after ordination to work in Vancouver Island. At the insistence of Amat, Lootens came to California and occupied several posts in the Diocese of Monterey-Los Angeles in the late 1860's. It is not unreasonable to assume that his election to the titular See of Castabala on March 3, 1868, and his appointment to the Vicariate Apostolic of Idaho and Montana was prompted by Amat's recommendation. Lootens invited Amat to San Francisco for the ceremonies of his consecration and he, together with Bishop Eugene O'Connell of Grass Valley, served as co-consecrators on August 9 when Archbishop Alemany raised Lootens to the episcopate.

Synodal activity occupied much of Amat's time during these years. A circular letter, bearing the bishop's seal, was sent to all the priests on February 28, 1862, announcing a diocesan synod which Amat had scheduled for the second Sunday after Easter. The notification directed that the prayer *Ad Postulandum Gratiam Spiritus Sancti* was to be recited at Mass each day until the conclusion of

---

[6]Archives of the Archdiocese of Baltimore (hereafter referred to as AAB), John McCloskey to Francis P. Kenrick, Rome, April 7, 1861.

the Synod, immediately before that already being said for the pope.[7] It had been exactly a decade since the first synod had been held in California under the auspices of Bishop Alemany and many new problems faced the Church which only a meeting of this nature could resolve. Fifteen priests were present for the solemn opening on May 4 of the first such gathering of this kind in Los Angeles. A primary concern of the fathers were the transitional problems resulting from the transfer from Mexican to American jurisdiction, together with a more precise definition of disciplinary laws not then in accordance with legislation of the councils of Baltimore. Much consideration was also given to matrimonial cases brought on by the large influx of non-Catholics into the southern part of the diocese. The matters of cemeteries and of secret societies likewise received attention as did the question of abstinence from meat on certain days. In regard to the last item, it should be pointed out that abstinence had been a troublesome problem for many years, indults having been sought and obtained at various times allowing the use of lard and other commodities in the preparation of foods consumed on Fridays. However, it was not until the 1880's that a final and satisfactory solution of the thorny problem was reached. In fact, parts of the Diocese of Tucson continued to partake of meat on days of abstinence until the middle 1950's, claiming for their justification an old papal indult given to Spain at the expulsion of the Moors.

Other matters faced the participants of the synod. Up to that time, thirteen parishes had been provided with priests, two new ones were in the process of formation with several others in the immediate planning stage. Still, the need for priests remained a paramount problem and

[7]AALA, *"Libro Gobierno,"* p. 37.

the bishop was vitally aware of it. On one occasion he said:

> From every part of this immense diocese, the people ask for
> priests to attend to their wants, but all in vain. There are no
> priests to be sent to them, there being only sixteen in all the
> diocese, a number quite insufficient to administer to the
> spiritual wants of the numerous Catholics, who live around
> the places of their residence.[8]

This plea was echoed in a letter to Martin J. Spalding,
Archbishop of Baltimore:

> . . . we labor under many difficulties, especially in regard to
> procuring a proper religious education to the youth, without
> which our labor is lost, this being the only hope left to us. We
> need for this purpose Religious Communities, whose members
> would devote themselves perseveringly to this object, being
> as missionaries must be, content with having aliments et qui-
> bus tegantur. . . . I feel inclined to expect that you could be
> the means and instrument to fill up this deficiency in the por-
> tion of the Lord's vineyard, confided to my care.[9]

A cordial response was received which opened the way to
further negotiations for religious communities coming to
the Diocese of Monterey-Los Angeles.[10] The bishop carefully outlined to Spalding the property agreement then in
vogue and its application to the various communities, lest
there be any misunderstanding on the matter.

One of the reasons for Amat's convoking of the synod
was his desire to consult his own priests about the forthcoming provincial council which Alemany formally announced on September 6. Thus when the meeting opened
in San Francisco on October 19, Amat was well prepared
to present the needs of the Church in Southern California

---

[8]Reprinted in the *Tidings,* December 8, 1939. Copy of a letter sent to Ireland
by Amat. No date or addressee was given in the reprint.

[9]AALA, Thaddeus Amat to Martin J. Spalding, Los Angeles, January 21, 1865.

[10]AAB, Thaddeus Amat to Martin J. Spalding, Los Angeles, April 22, 1865.

to this first provincial gathering.[11] Amat's typically judicious use of time is exemplified by his itinerary on the way to San Francisco. He travelled through the gold mining town of Aurora and then to Carson City making visitations and administering confirmation. Shortly after his arrival in the Bay City, he issued a circular letter[12] announcing the erection of an association authorized by Rome whose object, he said, was "the protection of the rights of the Holy See, attacked in these times by evil and impious men in order to obtain from heaven, through prayers and almsgiving, the assistance that the Vicar of Christ needs to govern the Church with freedom and independence." Amat urged his people to avail themselves of the indulgences and other privileges available to those promising to pray for the Holy Father during this time of trial. With the publication of his circular letter, Amat's attention was concentrated on the business of the provincial meeting which lasted for several days. It was the first such meeting and the bishops expressed the hope that it would set a precedent for future gatherings where the problems of the Church in California could be discussed.

One of Amat's methods of informing his people about meetings such as that held at San Francisco was the circulation of pastoral letters. On May 7, 1865,[13] he issued a letter calling attention to the approaching golden jubilee of Pope Pius IX's ordination and repeating his earlier request for prayers to sustain the Holy Father. Amat attributed the persecution of the pope to his strenuous position as the champion of truth and justice which had been the characteristic quality of his pontificate. In another

[11]Joseph S. Alemany to Thaddeus Amat, San Francisco, September 6, 1862.
[12]AALA, Circular, November 23, 1862.
[13]AALA, Thaddeus Amat, C.M., *Carta Pastoral* (Los Angeles, 1865).

pastoral, published early in 1869,[14] the bishop noted the appropriateness of directing "a few admonitions, regarding some of the principal points that may effect Christian obligation." His presentation of doctrine emphasized that the Church, as the guardian and depository of the faith must go forth not to a single point in the globe, but to the whole world, always preaching not to individuals but to everyone. In a tone reminiscent of our own day, Amat stated that the Church teaches not what is new but what is old and proven. She teaches what Christ teaches; her rules are His rules; her ways are Christ's ways. He went on to speak of the sad plight of the pope but pointed out that suffering seemed to be a characteristic of the rulers of Christendom. "There can be no true liberty, progress and civilization," he concluded, "without the fear of God and submission both to Him and to them by whom He governs the world in temporal and spiritual concerns."

The bishop used his pastoral to promulgate several of the earlier synodal decrees, noting the duties, not only of the laity but also of the clergy. "Your duties to them (pastors) are their rights, and their duties to you are also your rights." In the matter of the laity's generosity, he said he could not refrain from expressing sentiments of gratitude and praise for the zeal that some had shown in contributing to the poor and promoting the glory of God. And yet, he observed, poverty was still widespread and therefore, they had "only to look to the actual state of your churches throughout the Diocese and to the several localities which actually need a place of worship to see the needs that still face them."

[14]AALA, Thaddeus Amat, C.M., *Pastoral Letter* (Los Angeles, 1869).

Meanwhile Amat had summoned a second synod which met in Los Angeles on April 11, 1869.[15] Among other matters discussed was the drawing up of a diocesan catechism upon which to base the instruction of children. Many of the pastors were still using the old *doctrina* which had been so successful in mission days but whose usefulnes was clearly outdated. It had been prepared for strictly missionary areas and Southern California was gradually taking on a structure that set it apart from the earlier concepts of the friars. It was also decided at the synod that an annual collection should be taken up for the maintenance of diocesan orphanages which were experiencing anxiety because of their lack of funds. Amat asked for suggestions regarding the approaching Vatican Council, telling the priests that he would be their spokesman at the conclave later that year. One of the questions settled upon was that of stole fees,[16] which up to that time had not been regulated in the diocese. Amat set the general formula, which he later had printed for distribution, and originated the laudable custom of having all such fees accrue to the parishes and not the individual priests as was the observance in the eastern United States. The formal decree was not issued until July 1 as the bishop was anxious to compare it with a similar bulletin in the San Francisco area.

Amat's third synod convened in May, 1876,[17] in the Church of Our Lady of the Angels. It lasted until May 7 when the bishop imparted the apostolic blessing and adjourned the meeting. In addition to reaffirming the earlier decrees, the bishop officially extended to the diocese the regulations adopted at the provincial council recently held

[15]SBMA, III, 279. *Constitutions,* San Francisco, April 11-18, 1869.

[16]AALA, A chart in the hand of the Very Reverend Francis Mora and signed by Bishop Amat. Cf. also SBMA, III, 272.

[17]SBMA, III, 465, *Constitutions,* San Francisco, May 7, 1876.

at San Francisco. Several liturgical admonitions were contained in the statutes, most of which had not been enforced in earlier years because of the missionary status of the diocese. Nonetheless, Amat insisted that these observations were only becoming in a jurisdiction which had now risen to some degree of stability within the framework of the American Church.

Nor was Bishop Amat's knowledge of conciliar matters confined to California. On March 19, 1866, Archbishop Spalding asked him to submit a schema for the forthcoming plenary council which was scheduled to open at Baltimore on the first Sunday in October. As apostolic delegate to the council, Spalding was anxious to have opinions from the nation's bishops especially those versed in legal matters.[18] In July, Amat sent circulars out to all the priests of the diocese informing them of the coming council in Baltimore. The bishop announced his own plans to attend the council and requested that each parish begin a triduum for the fruitful deliberations of the fathers.[19] Shortly before leaving for Baltimore on July 25, Amat named Father Francis Mora, a fellow Catalonian, vicar general[20], conferring on him the same broad powers earlier given with papal approval to Father Blasius Raho. The *Sacramento* sailed from San Francisco on August 18 with Archbishop Alemany, Bishop Amat and Bishop Eugene O'Connell and three other priests. The voyage took them to Panama where they travelled overland and then up the Atlantic seaboard to New York.[21]

[18]John Lancaster Spalding, *op. cit.*, p. 195.
[19]AALA, *"Libro Gobierno,"* p. 53.
[20]*Ibid.*, p. 52.
[21]The *Monitor*, August 18, 1866.

The council formally opened on October 7. Several
items of the council's agenda pertained especially to the
Far West, including the recommendation of Alemany that
the Vicariate of Marysville be elevated to diocesan status.[22]
Of more immediate concern to Catholics in Southern California was the suggestion that a seminary[23] be set up in
Barcelona for the education of priests destined to labor
in Spanish-speaking areas of the United States. It was a
favorite project of Amat's and one on which he had been
working several years. He read a letter to the fathers from
Cardinal Barnabo endorsing the plan for a college in Barcelona. Nothing came of this idea at the time but this matter over a year later would come up again in Amat's correspondence with Spalding. He then said:

> If you thought proper, Most Reverend Archbishop, to devise
> some means by which this could come to the knowledge of the
> Prelates of these States as several of them labor under great
> difficulties for want of missionaries; and according to all ap-
> pearances, in Spain we could get a good supply, and without
> great expense. They could likewise be trained in a manner
> suitable for our missions; I doubt not, that some might be
> willing to join in the undertaking. . . .[24]

No definite action was taken by the bishops, however,
and the question remained in abeyance throughout Amat's
life. The fourth and last public session of the council was
held in Baltimore's historic Cathedral of the Assumption
on Sunday, October 21. A solemn Mass was celebrated by
Archbishop John Odin, C.M., of New Orleans attended
by President Andrew Johnson and several of his cabinet
members.

[22]This request was granted by Pius IX in a bull issued March 22, 1868. The
title of the new See was Grass Valley. Cf. Peter K. Guilday, *op. cit.,* p. 214.

[23]Cf. Appendix to *Acta et Decreta Concilii Plenarii Baltimorensis Tertii in
Ecclesia* . . . (Baltimore, 1884), letter dated November 13, 1867.

[24]AAB, Thaddeus Amat to Martin J. Spalding, Los Angeles, February 22, 1868.

Immediately after the council's adjournment Amat travelled the forty miles to Washington where he filed a claim against the government for rental—actually military occupation from 1849 to 1857—of the buildings of the missions at San Diego and San Luis Rey.[25] Apparently no results were forthcoming at that time although he had asked $8,000 from the War Department for the eight years of occupation, the reimbursement being based on the annual rental of each mission which he estimated to be worth $500.

The Bishop of Monterey-Los Angeles had previously made it known to his Vicar General that he planned to go on from New York to Rome for his *ad limina* visit,[26] it being also the nineteenth centenary of SS. Peter and Paul. Hence when his business was finished, he set out for the Eternal City where he made the usual calls at the various congregations and submitted his report to Propaganda. In his audience with Pope Pius IX he conveyed a spiritual bouquet gathered in his diocese in the pope's honor on the occasion of the latter's golden jubilee.[27] His reception was most cordial and the audience was concluded with the customary apostolic blessing for the bishop and his people. In October 1867, Amat stopped at All Hallows College where he recruited five more students for California.

While in Barcelona the previous year, Bishop Amat had expanded his earlier treatise on matrimony and had the new version printed in Spanish for use in California.[28] It was well received, perhaps more so than the English version which was a favorite of Archbishop Spalding. Later,

[25]The papers relating to this transaction are in the Hayes Collection which forms part of the Bancroft Library, Berkeley.

[26]AALA, "*Libro Gobierno*," p. 54.

[27]AALA, Thaddeus Amat, C.M., *Pastoral Letter* (San Francisco, 1870), p. 4.

[28]The Spanish title was *Tratado sobre del Matrimonio*.

Amat sent a copy of the Spanish version to the archbishop with these words:

> May I take the liberty of sending you by mail a copy of the translation of my treatise on marriage into Spanish, with the few alterations which you were so kind to remark to me. I hope you will be pleased with it and might help a little to facilitate the new impression in English, in case you intend to print it over again as you told me.[29]

The death of Father Gonzales Rubio on November 2, 1875,[30] the last of the old mission priests who had accompanied Garcia Diego to California in the early 1830's, deprived the Indians of their most vociferous spokesman, for Rubio never failed to champion the cause of the natives throughout his long and useful life. His refusal of the mitre of Baja California, and his forceful retention by the people at Santa Barbara when he was recalled to Zacatecas, were but two incidents that dramatized the high degree of respect in which he was held by the natives and townspeople of Santa Barbara and, for that matter, by all California. The great churchman was eulogized as,

> a noble man, a true Christian, very much respected and beloved by his people, and by all who knew him.[31]

Bancroft summed up the worth of Gonzales Rubio, the last survivor of the California missionaries as,

> a man respected and beloved by all from the beginning to the end of his career; one of the few Zacatecans who in ability, missionary zeal, and purity of life were equals to the Spanish Fernandinos.[32]

---

[29]AAB, Thaddeus Amat to Martin J. Spalding, Los Angeles, July 4, 1868.

[30]Los Angeles *Express,* November 15, 1875.

[31]William Heath Davis, *Sixty Years in California* (San Francisco, 1889), pp. 73-74.

[32]Hubert Howe Bancroft, *op. cit.,* III, 760.

Other calamities befell the diocese too. Vandalism was a great plague for the old mission buildings. Frequently the bishop was unable to hire caretakers to watch over the grounds which attracted mischievous youngsters and malicious vagrants who were frequently guilty of defiling the once sacred institutions. Considerable damage, for instance, was done at San Luis Rey near San Diego on October 6, 1868, so great in fact, that Bishop Amat wrote to Judge Hayes requesting legal assistance in order to prevent further damage. The justice decided that legal action would be costly and urged the bishop that an announcement in the local press would have a far more useful effect. With that in mind, Amat authorized the following notice to be inserted in some of the papers in the area:

> I have been requested by the Rt. Rev. T. Amat, Catholic Bishop of this Diocese, to give notice that he holds a patent for the buildings of the ex-Mission of San Luis Rey, in this county, and to warn all persons not to take away timbers, bricks or other material belonging thereto.[33]

Nonetheless, by the time the mission was again opened for service, most of its appurtenances had disappeared and even today small items are occasionally brought into the mission from nearby ranches where they have been hidden away for over a century.

Amat published another pastoral letter while visiting San Juan Bautista,[34] in which he announced certain "dispositions which the Holy Father deigned to make, with regard to our diocese. . . ."

> We had observed long since, and not without regret on our part, that some of our dear faithful, notwithstanding their good will and sincere desire to observe all the commandments of our Mother Church, whose observance, unless great ob-

---

[33]San Diego *Union,* October 10, 1868.

[34]AALA, Thaddeus Amat, C.M. *Pastoral Letter* (San Juan Bautista, 1870).

stacles should be in their way, is necessary for salvation, by reason of the difficult circumstances in which they were placed, they felt themselves depressed in mind, because they could not assist at the holy sacrifice of the Mass on certain festival days of obligation. We therefore entreated our Holy Father and Supreme Pastor that he might deign to provide, so as to quiet their consciences, with some mitigation in this respect, and also that we might thus, as much as the circumstances of the diocese allow, conform ourselves, as to the feasts of obligation and fasts, with the practice of the rest of the United States.[35]

Amat then went on to enumerate the privileges given by the pope. Among others he lessened the days of obligation by four and allowed certain others the days of precept to coincide with the normal Sunday observance. Fasting on the Saturdays of Advent was dispensed with and certain other minor obligations were suspended. Amat observed, however, that the people should remember that these privileges were granted "principally for the benefit of such persons whose circumstances of employment do not allow them to freely comply with the precept of the Church." He thus seemingly indicated that he expected those who were able to continue the existing practices.

The affection of his people was obvious on many occasions. For example, upon his return from the Vatican Council on December 16, 1870, a large group of people assembled at the station to greet him and to accompany him to the Church of Our Lady of the Angels where he sang a *Te Deum* for his safe arrival back in his diocese. Former Governor John G. Downey was among the welcoming party as were other prominent people of the city. Amat addressed the people in Spanish dwelling particularly on the disasters that had recently involved France

[35]*Ibid.*, p. 17.

and Spain. "In deploring the momentary triumph of the revolutionists," said a local reporter in summarizing the bishop's remarks, "who held those fine old Catholic countries as bleeding victims at their feet, he was so deeply affected as to shed copious tears." A formal greeting ceremony, held later in the bishop's residence, was the occasion of several speeches, among which that of Judge Jose Sepulveda was typical. He said:

> It becomes the rare privilege of my life to extend to you in the name of the citizens of Los Angeles, a welcome home. The unanimity with which this welcome is extended to you sufficiently manifests the high regard all classes have for you; it is only a meet tribute to the talents, virtue and piety which adorn your character.[36]

Other welcoming speeches were made and, said a local newspaperman:

> Many a devout person presented themselves to welcome him and to kiss the hand of him who is venerated as the common father of the faithful of this diocese.

As soon as he had settled down to his customary routine, Amat turned his attention to the problem of church titles. It had been a recurring problem and several of the religious communities had balked at his insistence on hold-the titles to their foundations. Nor was it clear to the civil authorities whether the actual *titulus* resided in the particular community occupying the area or in the diocese. This was especially confusing in regard to the mission property, which legally belonged only to the bishop but which, in many cases, was occupied by others. Amat had submitted the matter to Cardinal Barnabo some years previously, as well as to the Vincentian Superior General in Paris since the Daughters of Charity had also been affected by the

---

[36]Los Angeles *Star*, December 7, 1870.

regulation. The official interpretation of His Eminence, stated that "property in places of missions is to belong to the Missions but their use may be granted by the bishop to a society or congregation of priests."[37]

California law entered the discussion, too. Corporation sole, as viewed by the state, was the answer to the thorny problem and was to forestall a difficulty which faced the Church in the eastern part of the country for several decades, namely lay trusteeism. One student of the question has summarized the matter as follows:

> The American legal theory of corporation is fundamentally the same as that of English law. There can be no corporation which is not the creation of civil law, and all tenure of property likewise requires civil authority. The Church enjoys a large measure of freedom, but the law does not, within the United States, deal with it as such. The citizens of the United States however, in virtue of the federal and state constitutions, are free to practice their religion without interference, and where the state laws permit, to enter contractual agreement for the support of religion in a corporate capacity. Such corporations are controlled in the same manner as private corporations, and are subject to the principles of the common law.[38]

It was on February 27, 1854,[39] that Archbishop Alemany had recorded himself as corporation sole and, as such, became the principal spokesman for the Catholic Church in California in matters of property and disputes of legal title, a position which he continued to maintain after his promotion to the See of San Francisco.[40]

[37]ASMS, Thaddeus Amat to Jean-Baptiste Etienne, Los Angeles, July 13, 1864.

[38]Patrick J. Dignan, *A History of the Legal Incorporation of Catholic Church Property in the United States* (Washington, 1933), p. 208.

[39]*Ibid.,* pp. 246, 264.

[40]The incumbent Archbishop of San Francisco, who claims lineal episcopal succession from Archbishop Alemany, has traditionally acted in behalf of the California bishops in matters involving the several jurisdictions.

At the time of Amat's return from the Vatican Council he, too, registered himself as a corporation sole in the office of the recorder in Monterey County, this being done under the terms of an act of the state legislature approved[41] on May 4, 1852[42] and articles of incorporation were later filed with the county clerk of Monterey on June 13, 1876. Under previous legislation, especially that of 1850, the real estate which could be held by a religious corporation was limited to two whole lots in a town, or twenty acres in the country. The act of 1852 temporarily removed this restriction for corporaion sole, but in 1854 the legislature passed an amendment restoring the clause. This later amendment had validity until the adoption of section 602 of the civil code in 1878 when the limitation was removed on March 30:

> The present powers of corporation sole are those set forth in Sections 602, 602a, 602b, Civil Code. These include the power to buy, sell, lease or mortgage and in every way deal in real and personal property in the same manner that a natural person may.[43]

[41]Cf. Book C., p. 19, County Recorder of Monterey County, December 12, 1870.

[42]Cf. "Corporation Sole," Stat. 1852, p. 168, *Civil Code*, sec. 602. This amended, the earlier law of April 22, 1850, which read ". . . Whenever the rules of a society or church require for the management of estate and property thereof, it is made lawful for the bishop . . . to be a sole corporation. . . . For a proof of appointment of such bishop, it is made sufficient to record with the county clerk of the county in which the bishop resides, the letters of his appointment. . . ." For the entire text, cf. Theodore Hittell, *The General Laws of the State of California* (1850-1864), I, C. 8, Sec. 184.

[43]The Corporation Act of 1850 granted to every corporation the power:
   a. To have succession by its corporate name, for the period limited, and when no period is limited, perpetually;
   b. To sue and to be sued in any court;
   c. To make and use a common seal, and alter the same at its pleasure;
   d. To hold, purchase and convey such real and personal estate as the purposes of the corporation shall require, not exceeding the amount limited by law.

As one writer stated it:

> The corporation is not terminated or affected by the death or incompetency of the incumbent. Nor is an agency created by the corporation sole, such as a power of attorney, which in express terms provided that the agency shall not be terminated by a vacancy in the incumbency of the corporation, terminated by the death of the incumbent.[44]

A copy of the original articles,[45] duly certified by the county clerk of that county, was filed in the office of the clerk of Los Angeles on June 19, 1876. These articles were signed by Amat, who was then in Monterey, on December 9, 1870. He subscribed himself as the

> . . . Roman Catholic Bishop of Monterey duly constituted the Bishop of the Roman Catholic Church in the diocese of Monterey in the State of California . . . the rules, regulations and discipline of the Roman Catholic Church in the United States of America require it for the administration of the temporalities of the said Roman Catholic Church in the said Diocese, and the management of the estate and property of the said Church.[46]

It should be noted that the older title of the diocese was used in these official documents and not the later one with its addition of 'Los Angeles,' dating from July 7, 1859. This was done to safeguard titles to the mission buildings and lands which had been awarded to Bishop Alemany, as the Ordinary of Monterey in December of 1855.

Upon Bishop Amat's return to California late in 1870, he gave every appearance of being in his typically robust health. It was only with Father Mora's departure for Europe the next year[47] that the first indication of fatigue be-

---

[44]Dale G. Vaughn, *El Obispo* (Los Angeles, 1929), p. 4.

[45]I.e., those recorded in the Monterey County Records, December 12, 1870.

[46]Vaughn, *op. cit.*, p. 5.

came apparent for the added duties which fell on his shoulders during the absence of his vicar general weakened him considerably. The additional activity told on his health as he himself later admitted.

In the fall, after Mora's return unmistakable indications of a decline in the bishop's health could no longer be disguised and by the spring it was evident that measures would be necessary to secure the efficient working order of the diocese. Amat confided in Archbishop Alemany and was advised by the metropolitan to ask for a coadjutor. When this action was taken, the pope readily granted the petition and instructed the bishops of the province to send in the *terna*. A meeting of the California bishops was held and a list was drawn up of available candidates for submission to Rome. Alemany conveyed the result of the bishops' action to John B. Purcell, Archbishop of Cincinnati:

> The Holy Father having allowed that a Coadjutor may be given to Bishop Amat, who suffers occasionally in bad health, the Bishops of this Province met yesterday and unanimously commended to the S. Congregation, as fit for this office, the three following priests: 1. Very Rev. Francis Mora, Vic. Gen. of Bp. Amat; 2. Rev. Vincent Vinyes, O.S.D. of the Convent of Benecia, Cal.; 3. Very Rev. James McGill, Priest of the Congregation of the Mission.[48]

The obvious choice of the bishops was the Reverend Francis Mora who had been a priest of the diocese for sixteen years and vicar general for seven. Southern California with its new and growing population, most of whom

[47]Father Mora went to Spain in order to bring back the Sisters of the Immaculate Heart of Mary. The sisters arrived in San Francisco on Angust 31 and were immediately assigned to Gilroy and San Juan Bautista abandoned by the Daughters of Charity during Amat's absence in Rome.

[48]Archives of the University of Notre Dame (hereafter referred to as AUND), Joseph S. Alemany to John Purcell, San Francisco, January 30, 1873.

were of a non-Spanish origin, posed several problems, most important of which was the language barrier. The Catholics of the city were no more than half native now while those of San Bernardino were also drawn heavily from the new migration; and even San Diego was profiting by the growth. On the other hand, Santa Barbara, San Buenaventura and other places remained mostly Spanish-speaking, and all considerations being duly weighed, it was thought advisable to select a man who could easily attend to the spiritual needs of both classes. Both Father Mora and Father Vinyes were conversant in English and Spanish and it was Alemany's opinion that Vinyes might well be the abler. He then told Purcell, "But as Father Mora has been many years by the side of Bp. Amat and a good gentle, and prudent priest, we have joined in praying that he may be the coadjutor."[49] Bishop Amat's personal choice was Mora and it was Mora's name which the bishops proposed to the Holy Father as their first choice for position.

The nomination met with no objection in Rome and the bulls appointing Francis Mora titular Bishop of Mosnopolis and coadjutor with the right of succession to Monterey-Los Angeles, were dated May 20, 1873. News of their issuance reached Los Angeles early the next month and was received enthusiastically by both clergy and laity. In view of the precarious state of Amat's health, the consecration was scheduled for Sunday, August 3. Great preparations were made by the Catholics of the city who were especially fond of Mora whom they had grown to love and respect over the years. Mora asked Bishop Amat to officiate and he requested Archbishop Alemany and Bishop O'Connell to

---

[49]*Ibid.*

act as co-consecrators. One columnist expressed the current sentiment in these words:

> The consecration of a Catholic Bishop ever has been one of the most imposing ceremonies of the Church. On Sunday last, a priest who has long lived amongst us in and quietly endeared himself in a very special way to all with whom he has come in contact, was elevated to the higher dignity of the Episcopal Chair. The growing importance of this Diocese, its large extent, and the impossibility of its being presided over effectually by one Diocesan, has led the Right Reverend Bishop Amat to beg the appointment of a Bishop Coadjutor to assist and strengthen him in his labors. The appointment of Father Mora and his selection from the three names submitted to the Holy Father, is understandably a wise one and we are sure that there is no one in Los Angeles today who does not rejoice in the great dignity conferred upon him.[50]

The ceremonies began at nine o'clock in the morning and long before the appointed hour, the Church of Our Lady of the Angels was filled with the admirers and friends of the bishop-elect. Father Michael Duran read the bulls of appointment authorizing the consecration and the oath of office was administered. After the ceremony itself was concluded, the two bishops concelebrated Holy Mass. It was a memorable occasion in the City of the Angels, the first in its history; and it would be a half century before a similar ceremony would again take place in Los Angeles. The sermon was preached by Archbishop Alemany who took his text from the twenty-eighth chapter of the *Acts of the Apostles*. It was a sermon "as only the archbishop can preach on an occasion when his heart is gladdened, his emotions unusually heightened." After the Mass, a luncheon was served during which Judge Sepulveda and other distinguished personages paid their respects to the new bishop. Mora was to prove a great sup-

[50]Los Angeles *Star*, August 5, 1873.

port to Amat during his declining years and much of the diocesan administration was handed over to the new bishop. For the first time in his long missionary career, Amat began to feel somewhat relieved of the greater burdens of his ministry. He continued to preside on certain feastdays and never left any doubt as to his own position as ordinary of the diocese but it was the beginning of a transition which the old Vincentian was happy to see approaching.

Amat wrote two more pastorals during these years.[51] One in April of 1872 dealt with the "universal corruption, which threatens the very foundations of Christian society, especially in Europe." Amat attributed the cause of the general world depravity to "the want of faith, which as the Council of Trent says: is the fundament and root of justification." The bishop went on to condemn in no uncertain words the activity of secret societies operating within the diocese which, he said, "monopolize every branch of enterprise in the country." In their place, he advised the laity to affiliate with one or another of the Catholic associations recommended by the pope since these latter were, by their very nature, subject to ecclesiastical authority. The second of these pastorals, dated November 30, 1873, was addressed to the clergy and reiterated an allocution of Pius IX to which these words were added: "History teaches us, that this (world-wide persecution) is scarcely an abnormal condition of the Church. It has been persecuted in the past ages, and will be persecuted until the end of time. It is a part of that flood of pride, falsehood, disobedience, lawlessness, iniquity and immorality which has never ceased. . . ."

[51]AALA, Thaddeus Amat, C.M., *Pastoral Letter* (Los Angeles, 1872 and 1873).

On March 14, 1874, Archbishop Alemany announced the convocation of the Second Provincial Council of San Francisco[52] which would meet in the Bay City in late April. The four bishops of the province were directed to draw up lists of prospective decrees which would be submitted for action. Among others offered by Amat were the following:

> 1st . . . We should make a decree about the conditions for ordinations; the oath that the ordinands are to take expressing the things to which they bind themselves, of remaining in the diocese, and not entering a Religious Order, without being dispensed by the Holy See; 2nd . . . A decree expressing the Disposition of the Holy See concerning the Sisters of Charity and other Communities (Religious) with regard to the way of holding property, indicating the communities affected by its exceptions; 3rd . . . A decree establishing uniformity with regard to the way of granting or refusing dispensations, conditions for granting them or refusing; 4th . . . A decree concerning secret societies declaring which are to be held as such and which not, precautions to be taken when there is not certainty about their being lawful or not, and penalties for the transgressors of said decree.[53]

Both Bishop Amat and Bishop Mora attended the meeting. At the conclusion of the council, a pastoral letter was issued to the clergy and laity of the province which took cognizance of the woes of the Church of Europe. The bishops said:

> The attitude of some rulers of the world toward the Church of Christ is also a subject of continual sorrow to us as we feel confident it must be of deep regret to you. Unmindful of their duties and obligations as the guardians of the principles of human justice—of the rights and liberties of others, and of that submission due by all to divinely constituted Church authority, they have in several instances . . . sacrilegiously

[52]SBMA, III, 375, Joseph S. Alemany to clergy, San Francisco, March 14, 1874.
[53]AALA, "Decrees to be Proposed," in hand of Thaddeus Amat.

confiscated the possessions of the faithful—set at naught the authority of the Supreme Pastor. . . .[54]

The well written and scholarly treatise, composed almost entirely by Archbishop Alemany, also treated of matrimony, dwelling especially on the dangers of mixed marriages. Finally, there were warm words of praise and gratitude to the priests of the province:

> We take this occasion to say that we are not unacquainted with the zeal, ardor and devotion displayed by them (our venerable brethren in the Ministry) in the discharge of the duties of the sacred Ministry. It is, indeed, to us the source of the greatest comfort; from it we derive the brightest consolations, that we are aided in the work of the Lord by so zealous and such efficient coadjutors.[55]

In view of Amat's failing health it was thought by his physician that a trip to Europe might be advantageous. Accordingly, the bishop left Los Angeles late in 1874 and travelled through the continent to his native Barcelona and Vich[56] where he rested and hoped for a return of health, which never came. He journeyed to Paris on his way back and stopped for treatment at the mineral baths of Vichy.[57] By the time he reached the United States in the Summer of 1875, he realized there would be no permanent recovery. His arrival in New York[58] was warmly reported by some of the papers which raised the hope that he would soon be active again. Amat went first to San Francisco where he spent some time with the archbishop before returning to Los Angeles.[59]

[54]SBMA, III, 378, *Pastoral Letter,* May 3, 1874, p. 4.

[55]*Ibid.,* p. 15.

[56]AUND, Thaddeus Amat to Charles Cerves, Vich, March 22, 1875.

[57]ASMS, Thaddeus Amat to Superior General, Los Angeles, November 4, 1875.

[58]Amat arrived on June 20th according to the New York *Herald.*

[59]AUND, Thaddeus Amat to Charles Cerves, Los Angeles, October 18, 1875.

The cause of Amat's original illness is not known although he believed that "to a great extent the debts that weighed me down were the cause of my illness for which reason I went to Europe during the past year."[60] In any event he put himself under the care of Dr. Manuel Fernandez and the physician later reported that the bishop's memory was occasionally impaired, an indication that he may have sustained several minor strokes prior to 1876. He also suffered intermittently from asthma which had weakened his heart. A separate diagnosis of Amat's illness was made by Dr. William Jones of San Francisco on October 25, 1877. His report indicated that the bishop's heart and lungs were normal but that there were some signs of advancing age. Dr. Jones said:

> My examination was as much directed to the ascertainment of his mental as of his physical condition. He was quite corpulent and I discovered a tendency to paralysis or apoplexy. Though my efforts were especially directed to that purpose, I could detect no defect in his memory. He told me, however, that he could not remember recent events as well as those of an earlier period. I did not regard such circumstances as strange in a person of his age. I could discover no impairment of the reflective faculties, his judgment or reason. He was fully competent for the transaction of business.[61]

Bishop Mora was able to report to Alemany in November that Amat "continues improving in his health."[62] Nonetheless, the bishop revised his will on November 19, 1877, in favor of his coadjutor with all the legal formalities.[63]

[60]SBMA, III, 443, Thaddeus Amat to Jose Romo, Los Angeles, September 27, 1875.

[61]AALA, Written report of the bishop's health. Source unknown.

[62]AALA, Francis Mora to Joseph S. Alemany, Los Angeles, November 27, 1877.

[63]Bishop Amat had executed wills in favor of Archbishop Alemany on October 16, 1856 and March 27, 1866. He changed them in favor of Bishop Francis Mora in 1873. His final treatment was dated November 19, 1877.

The end came suddenly. Shortly after one o'clock on Sunday, May 12, 1878, Thaddeus Amat was seized by a fatal heart attack. Despite the gradual disintegration of his health, the news came as a shock to the clergy and laity of the diocese. He had appeared in excellent spirits the preceding day and had even discussed several important business matters with Bishop Mora. In the afternoon, he took his customary ride in the carriage with apparently little discomfort.[64] Immediately upon Amat's death, Bishop Mora succeeded to the see and began at once to arrange for the funeral obsequies of his beloved predecessor. He telegraphed Archbishop Alemany and asked him to sing the funeral Mass. Alemany answered immediately that he would be present for the occasion. Special messages were dispatched to the pope, the Archbishop of Baltimore and to the priests of the diocese.[65] Amat's remains were laid in state in the Church of Our Lady of the Angels in a handsome glass-covered metallic casket. Calla lilies and leaves of myrtle were banked by his loving people around the catafalque bearing the dead shepherd. Great crowds of the faithful filed into the church to view, for the final time, the man whom they had known and loved so long as their bishop.

Promptly at ten o'clock on May 14, the funeral cortege came to a halt before Saint Vibiana's Cathedral, already filled to capacity with mourners. The venerable metropolitan, visibly shaken by the loss of his long-time friend, was helped up the steps by Bishop Mora and Father Hugh Gallagher. Priests, sisters, students, city officials, laity had come to pay their final respects. Six priests carried the flower-draped casket into the cathedral and placed it on a

[64]Los Angeles *Express,* May 13, 1878.
[65]AALA. Printed notice of Amat's death, Los Angeles, May 12, 1878.

porte-mort in front of the chancel rail. At the conclusion of the Mass, Amat's remains were lowered into the vault beneath the sanctuary of the church, first and only person ever buried in the edifice.[66]

EPILOGUE

Amat filled admirably the threefold office of teacher, priest and king. That he was always the *teacher* is obvious enough for even the rapid growth of his diocese, its needs of churches and schools, together with all the other pressing responsibilities of administering such a vast expanse of territory, never distracted Amat from those intellectual pursuits to which he had a natural proclivity. His scholarly *Treatise on Matrimony* is one indication of the multiphased talents of the Lazarist missionary. The sixty-nine page book, outlined in great detail the duties and obligations of marital life. His long experience as a seminary professor brought about a book as well received by the American hierarchy as it was by his most simple diocesans. If Amat was proficient in the written word, he was no less a teacher in the spoken word. And although it was said of him that "he speaks correctly but with the accent of a stranger,"[67] he was in constant demand as an orator. One of his most memorable sermons was given in Saint Mary's Cathedral at San Francisco on the occasion of Archbishop Alemany's silver jubilee in 1875.[68] Dwelling on the progress of the Church in California and the debt due the gentle Dominican friar responsible for so much of that

[66]The remains of Bishop Amat were exhumed on November 30, 1962 and found to be substantially incorrupt. They were reinterred in the episcopal vault at Calvary Mausoleum.

[67]Archives of the Santa Barbara County Historical Society, "Diary of Judge Charles C. Huse."

[68]Thomas Denis McSweeney, *op. cit.,* p. 37.

success, Amat eloquently praised the man under whose administration "The Church has fairly distanced all her competitors in this field of religious rivalry."[69] Of the silent word, that of good example, sometimes thought the most persuasive and effective type of teaching, one typical account is that of a missionary priest who first saw the bishop in 1854. He was, as he says, "charmed with (Amat's) sweet simplicity and extreme goodness of heart" and thought the bishop's arrival could mean nothing other than "an immense good" for California.[70]

That the Bishop of Monterey-Los Angeles was a good and humble *priest* is seen in the utter horror he had of earthly honors. His repugnance to accepting the episcopate grew out of this attitude and he was heard on several occasions to echo the sentiments of Robert Bellarmine who expressed to a well-wisher these words on his nomination to the cardinalate:

> These things are wonderful and great, if we cleave to earth and forget our true country. But if we judge aright, like good scholars of the school of Christ, if we have studied with attention the Gospels and Saint Paul, if we seriously consider ourselves strangers and pilgrims on earth, what are all these things but a cloud that appears for a little time, and what is our life but grass, and what is its glory but a flower to the field? I certainly, dearest Father, can make this confession to your paternal heart that I never set any value on the purple, and now, so far from valuing it, I rather marvel greatly at those who do. I pity them too, for they seem not to care for the glory of the Eternal King if only they may gain some fleeting, counterfeit honors and the shadow of renown.[71]

*King*ship in the Church is expressed by the jurisdiction a priest holds over his people. In this regard we are told

[69]P. J. Thomas, *Our Centennial Memoir* (San Francisco, 1877), p. 163.
[70]*Annales de la Propagation de la Foi* (Paris, 1858), p. 67. Edmund Venisse to n.n., Chile, 1856.
[71]James Broderick, S.J., *Robert Bellarmine, 1542-1621* (New York, 1950), I, 406.

that Amat was a "rigid disciplinarian" while remaining always "a just man."[72] On the whole Amat ruled wisely and wherever there was a show of opposition, it was no reflection on his character but due rather to the vicissitudes which every bishop experiences in the government of his diocese. Even his frequent disagreements with Alemany melt away when the archbishop says that "without his aid and counsel, what was hopefully started, might have died an early death."

Thaddeus Amat was a plain and humble man, a well-disciplined priest, and a man of deep personal convictions. He lived in the spirit of the Vincentian rule from the time he joined the community as a novice until his death as a member of the American hierarchy. Amat had by nature a quick-tempered disposition, but he rarely manifested either dejection or anxiety. The charm of his character, his deep but unostentatious piety, his outward dignity, would ennoble human nature in any profession, but they dignified it with a peculiar grace in the person of this Catholic bishop.

The vigor and enthusiastic energy of his younger days and the resources latent in his strong personality came into play in all his actions and remained in evidence until he brought his large and rough missionary diocese out of the near chaos in which he found it to the status at the time of his death of a neatly organized ecclesiastical jurisdiction. The notable development of the diocese under his direction was a reflection of his ability and worth.

What Bishop Amat accomplished in California may be summarized under four broad features which were particularly noteworthy. In the first place, there was the diplomatic but firm handling of the delicate Franciscan con-

[72]John Rothensteiner, *op. cit.,* I, 837.

troversy. Secondly, the wisdom of his insistence on a system of Catholic education in the diocese at a time when others considered it a mere velleity, was later borne out; thirdly, the erection of Saint Vibiana's Cathedral deserves special note for it was a major event in the Los Angeles of the 1870's, and even today it stands as the oldest non-mission church in the city; finally, there was the establishment of a diocesan curia which had been lacking under Amat's two predecessors.

That such a man as Thaddeus Amat was popular with strong and enduring popularity that captivates the heart and mind rather than the fancy, was inevitable, and the love and admiration of his people on special occasions, such as his return from Europe in 1870 was almost unknown in Los Angeles history. Amat was a true pioneer, a man whose whole life was dedicated to the *ars artium, regimen animarum*. The writer believes he deserves to have his story told and he hopes that this study may have satisfactorily captured the life of a man, who until now, has been largely ignored by historians of the American Church.

CLERGY IN THE MONTEREY DIOCESE — ANNO DOMINI, 1854

Name	Status	Nationality	Station
Rev. Doroteo Ambris	Secular	Mexico	San Antonio
Rev. Peter Bagaria	Secular	Spain	San Juan Capistrano
Rev. John Camapla	Secular	Gerona	Santa Ines
Rev. John Comellas	Secular	Spain	Santa Cruz
Rev. Sebastian Filoteo	Secular	Mexico	Monterey
Rev. Michael Gomez	Secular	Mexico	San Luis Obispo
Rev. Antonio Jimeno	Franciscan	Mexico	Santa Barbara
Rev. Jose Jimeno	Franciscan	Mexico	Santa Barbara
Rev. Anacletus Lestrada	Picpus	France	Los Angeles
Rev. John Molinier	Secular	France	San Juan Bautista
Rev. Francis Rogalle	Secular	France	San Buenaventura
Adm. Rev. Gonzales Rubio	Franciscan	Mexico	Santa Barbara
Rev. Francisco Sanchez	Franciscan	Mexico	Santa Barbara
Rev. Edmund Venisse	Picpus	France	Los Angeles

RECAPITULATION

Priests in Diocese... 14
Churches with Resident Pastors........................... 11
Pastorates Vacant 1
Churches Abandoned 5*

*San Luis Rey, San Fernando, La Purisima, San Miguel and Nuestra Señora de Soledad.

CLERGY OF THE MONTEREY-LOS ANGELES DIOCESE IN 1878

Name	Date of Ordination or Arrival	Death
1. Rev. Joachim Adam	Came on December 2, 1863	July 31, 1907
2. Rev. Valentine Aguilera	Ordained June 29, 1872	February 24, 1908
3. Rev. Francis Alvarez, O.S.F.	Came in 1872	July 10, 1897
4. Rev. Doroteo Ambris	Ordained January 1, 1846	February 5, 1883
5. Rev. Joachim Bot	Ordained June 29, 1862	August 13, 1903
6. Rev. Peter Carrasco	Ordained March 12, 1876	March 27, 1924
7. Rev. Angel Cassanova	Came in 1860	March 11, 1893
8. Rev. Valentine Closa	Came September 30, 1870	March 9, 1916
9. Rev. Francis Codina, O.S.F.	Came in August, 1860	Left in 1887
10. Rev. Hugh Curran	Came October 16, 1866	November 29, 1917
11. Rev. Denis Delaney, C.M.	Ordained August 12, 1877	December 22, 1884
12. Rev. Michael Duran	Came in 1860	October 29, 1889
13. Rev. Philip Farrely	Came October 24, 1868	May 16, 1916
14. Rev. Victor Fauron	Came in 1872	January of 1887
15. Rev. Joseph Galera	Came in May, 1873	November 14, 1878
16. Rev. Bernard Gelss	Came December 9, 1874	June 8, 1880
17. Rev. Joseph Godiol, O.S.F.	Ordained 1856	October 30, 1901
18. Rev. Patrick Hawe	Came September 25, 1872	August 30, 1923
19. Rev. Thomas Hudson	Came October 14, 1864	June 10, 1907
20. Rev. Michael Lynch	Came October 3, 1872	August 11, 1903
21. Rev. Michael Mahony	Came October 16, 1866	June 24, 1901
22. Rev. Martin Marron	Ordained March 12, 1876	March 16, 1905
23. Rt. Rev. Francis Mora	Ordained March 19, 1856	August 3, 1905
24. Rev. Joseph Mut	Ordained June 29, 1862	October 1, 1889
25. Rev. Hugh McNamee	Came September 27, 1873	October 3, 1902
26. Rev. Maurice O'Brien, C.M.	Came in 1866	October 22, 1890
27. Rev. John O'Donnell	Came in 1877	Left December 21, 1880
28. Rev. John Pujol	Came September 30, 1870	October 30, 1921
29. Rev. Michael Richardson, C.M.	Ordained June 26, 1869	December 8, 1920
30. Adm. Rev. Joseph Romo, O.S.F.	Came in 1872	circa 1891
31. Rev. Apollinaris Roussel	Came in 1857	January 25, 1891
32. Adm. Rev. Michael Rubi, C.M.	Ordained March 25, 1858	October 8, 1907
33. Rev. Cyprian Rubio	Ordained March 19, 1856	August 15, 1905
34. Rev. Francis Sanchez, O.S.F.	Ordained in 1838	April 7, 1884
35. Rev. Cornelius Scannell	Came December 10, 1870	October 2, 1913
36. Rev. Frederic Schots		
37. Adm. Rev. Cajetan Sorrentini	Came in 1854	June 30, 1893
38. Rev. Polydore Stockman	Came in December, 1873	July 16, 1924
39. Rev. Anthony Ubach	Ordained in March, 1860	March 26, 1907
40. Rev. Peter Verdaguer	Ordained June 29, 1862	October 26, 1911
41. Rev. James Vila	Ordained in 1855	October 20, 1895

RECAPITULATION OF CLERGY IN DIOCESE

Diocesan priests 31
Regular priests 10
Total priests 41

DIOCESAN ORDINATIONS DURING BISHOP AMAT'S EPISCOPATE

MARCH 19, 1856—Rt. Rev. Thaddeus Amat, C.M.

1. Rev. Francis Mora....................Died in Spain, August 3, 1905*
2. Rev. Cyprian Rubio..............Died in Los Angeles, August 15, 1905
3. Rev. Vincent Llover.........Returned to Spain in 1863. No other record
4. Rev. Dominic Serrano...............Died in Spain, September 27, 1890
5. Rev. Benedict Capdevila..........Died in Los Angeles, October 31, 1861

MARCH OF 1860—Most Rev. Joseph S. Alemany, O.P.

6. Rev. Anthony Ubach...............Died in San Diego, March 26, 1907

DECEMBER 12, 1862—Rt. Rev. Thaddeus Amat, C.M.

7. Rev. Joseph Mut...........................Died on October 1, 1889
8. Rev. Joachim Bot..........................Died on August 13, 1903
9. Rev. Peter Verdaguer.................Died in Texas, October 26, 1911†
10. Rev. Vincent Riera...................Left Diocese in February of 1864

OCTOBER 3, 1869—Rt. Rev. Thaddeus Amat, C.M.

11. Rev. Philip Farrelly............................Died on May 16, 1916

JUNE 29, 1872—Rt. Rev. Thaddeus Amat, C.M.

12. Rev. Valentine Aguilera.........Died near Barcelona, February 24, 1908
13. Rev. Valentine Closa.............................Died March 9, 1916
14. Rev. James Pujol..............Died in San Francisco, February 26, 1874
15. Rev. John Pujol..............................Died October 30, 1921
16. Rev. John Prat................Died in Los Angeles, September 16, 1876

MARCH 25, 1874—Rt. Rev. Francis Mora

17. Rev. Polydore Stockman...........................Died July 16, 1924

MARCH 12, 1876—Rt. Rev. Francis Mora

18. Rev. Martin Marron...................Died at San Jose, March 16, 1905
19. Rev. Peter Carrasco.............................Died March 27, 1924

---

*Consecrated Coadjutor Bishop of Monterey-Los Angeles, August 3, 1873.
†Consecrated Vicar Apostolic of Brownsville, November 9, 1890.

FUNCTIONING ECCLESIASTICAL FOUNDATIONS IN 1878

Title	Origin	Area	Condition	Status
San Diego de Alcala	1769	San Diego	Abandoned	Attended from San Diego
San Carlos Borromeo	1770	Monterey	Church	Parish
San Antonio de Padua	1771	Jolon	Church	Parish
San Gabriel Arcangel	1771	San Gabriel	Church	Parish
San Carlos Borromeo	1771	Carmel	Abandoned	Attended from Monterey
San Luis Obispo	1772	S. Luis Obispo	Church	Parish
San Juan Capistrano	1776	Capistrano	Church	Parish
Purisima Concepcion	1780	Fort Yuma	Station	Attended from Arizona City
San Buenaventura	1782	Ventura	Church	Parish
Santa Barbara	1786	Sta. Barbara	Convent	Non-parochial
Holy Cross	1791	Santa Cruz	Church	Parish
Soledad	1791	Soledad	Station	Attended from Salinas
San Juan Bautista	1797	San Juan	Church	Parish
San Fernando	1797	San Fernando	Church	Attended from Los Angeles
San Miguel	1797	San Miguel	Church	Attended fr. S. Luis Obispo
San Luis Rey	1798	San Luis Rey	Church	Attended from Capistrano
Santa Ines	1804	Solvang	Church	Parish
San Bernardino Asis.	1810	S. Bernardino	Church	Parish
San Antonio de Padua	1816	Pala	Church	Attended from Capistrano
Santa Ysabel Asis.	1818	San Diego	Station	Attended from San Diego
Our Lady of the Angels	1822	Los Angeles	Church	Parish
San Pascual	1834	San Diego Co.	Chapel	Attended from San Diego
Santos Reyes	1833	King's River	Station	Attended from Visalia
Saint Francis	1839	Camulos	Station	Attended from Ventura
San Salvador	1854	Jurupa	Church	Attended fr. S. Bernardino
Our Lady of Sorrows	1856	Sta. Barbara	Church	Parish
Immaculate Heart	1857	Pajaro	Church	Parish
Our Lady of Mt. Carmel	1857	Montecito	Chapel	Attended by Franciscans
Immaculate Conception	1859	San Diego	Church	Parish
San Jose	1859	Los Angeles Co.	Chapel	Attended from San Gabriel
San Antonio de Padua	1859	Santa Ana	Station	Attended from Anaheim
Saint Boniface	1860	Anaheim	Church	Parish
Nativity of B.V.M.	1860	Visalia	Church	Parish
Saint Patrick	1861	Watsonville	Church	Parish
Saint Joseph	1862	Havilah City	Chapel	Attended from Visalia
San Ramon	1864	Santa Maria	Station	Attended from Santa Ines
Our Lady of Mt. Carmel	1864	Panocha	Station	Attended from San Juan
Millerton	1864	Fresno County	Station	Attended from Visalia
Saint Peter	1865	Wilmington	Chapel	Attended from Los Angeles
Saint Clare	1866	Rio Sta. Clara	Station	Attended from Ventura
Saint Mary	1866	Gilroy	Church	Parish
Saint Isidore	1867	Guadalupe	Station	Attended from Santa Ines
Santa Rosa	1869	Cambria Pines	Chapel	Attended fr. S. Luis Obispo

FUNCTIONING ECCLESIASTICAL FOUNDATIONS IN 1878

Title	Origin	Area	Condition	Status
Our Lady of Refuge	1869	Castroville	Church	Parish
Our Lady of Guadalupe	1871	Sotoville	Church	Attended from Salinas
San Jacinto	1871	S. Bernard. Co.	Station	Attended fr. S. Bernardino
Temascal	1871	S. Bernard. Co.	Station	Attended fr. S. Bernardino
San Jose de Arriba	1871	Los Angeles Co.	Station	Attended from San Gabriel
Carpinteria	1872	S. Barbara Co.	Station	Attended by Franciscans
Saint Joseph	1874	San Diego	Church	Attended from San Diego
Ganzales	1875	Monterey Co.	Station	Attended from Salinas
Bakersfield		Bakersfield	Station	Attended from Visalia
Our Lady of Mt. Carmel	1875	Aptos	Chapel	Attended from Santa Cruz
Tulare	1875	Tulare	Station	Attended from Visalia
Sierrita	1875	S. Bernardino	Station	Attended fr. S. Bernardino
Saint Timothy	1875	San Timoteo	Chapel	Attended fr. S. Bernardino
Saint Vibiana Cathedral	1876	Los Angeles	Church	Non-parochial
Immaculate Conception	1876	Lompoc	Church	Attended from Santa Ines
Saint James	1876	Pauma	Station	Attended from Capistrano
Cerro Gordo	1876	Inyo County	Station	Attended from Visalia
Lone Pine	1876	Inyo County	Station	Attended from Visalia
Independence	1876	Inyo County	Station	Attended from Visalia
Sacred Heart	1876	Salinas	Church	Parish
Sacred Heart	1877	Hollister	Church	Attended from San Juan
La Palera	1877	S. Barbara Co.	Station	Attended by Franciscans
Santa Monica	1877	Santa Monica	Station	Attended from Los Angeles
Fresno	1878	Fresno	Station	Attended from Visalia

RECAPITULATION

Churches 30
Public Chapels 8
Stations 26
Abandoned Missions 2
Convent-Novitiate 1
Private Oratories 7
Parishes 20

(Date of origin refers to earliest designation, as mission, asistencia, station, chapel or church. The title given is that used in 1878.)

BIBLIOGRAPHY

(This bibliography is not presented as an exhaustive enumeration and includes only those works which were especially serviceable in the preparation of this treatise.)

I. Archival Sources:

Archives of the Archdiocese of Baltimore (AAB).
Archives of the Archdiocese of Los Angeles (AALA).
Archives of the Archdiocese of San Francisco (AASF).
Archives of Juventudes de la Medella Milagrosa (AJMM).
Archives de la Maison-Mere des Lazaristas (AMM).
Archives of Mary Immaculate Seminary (AMIS).
Archives of the Sacred Congregation of Propaganda Fide (APF).
Archives of Saint Charles Seminary, Overbrook.
Archives of Saint Mary-of-the-Assumption Church, Perryville.
Archives of Saint Mary's Seminary, Perryville (ASMS).
Archives of Saint Vincent's Church, Saint Louis.
Archives of the University of Notre Dame (AUND).
Papers of Francis X. Reuss, Overbrook.
Santa Barbara Mission Archives (SBMA).

II. Unpublished Works:

Baggot, Sister M. Reginald, I.H.M., "The California Institute of the Most Holy and Immaculate Heart of the Blessed Virgin Mary," (unpublished Master's dissertation, University of Southern California, 1937).

Easterly, Frederick J., C.M., "The Foundation of the Vincentians in the United States, (1816-1835)," (unpublished Master's dissertation, The Catholic University of America, 1936).

II. Unpublished Works *(Continued)*:

Eberhardt, Newman C., C.M., "Right Reverend Thaddeus Amat, C.M.," (article submitted to the New Catholic Encyclopedia, 1961).

Edwards, James, C.M., "Vincentian Educational Institutions in the United States," (unpublished Master's dissertation, The Catholic University of America, 1925).

Hague, Harland, "A History of Religion in Southern California, 1846-1880," (unpublished Master's dissertation, Columbia University, 1958.)

Hessel, Josephine A., "The History of the Catholic Church in Los Angeles," (unpublished Master's dissertation, University of Southern California, 1937).

III. Newspapers:

Alta California (San Francisco).

Catholic Telegraph and Advocate.

El Ancora de Barcelona.

El Clamor Publico (Los Angeles).

Giornale di Roma.

Gilroy *Gazette.*

Los Angeles *Daily News.*

Los Angeles *Express.*

Los Angeles *Republican.*

Los Angeles *Star.*

Leader (Baltimore).

Monitor (San Francisco).

North American and United States Gazette (Philadelphia).

New York *Freeman's Journal and Catholic Register.*

The *Pacific.*

Osservatore Romano.

Sacramento *Bee.*

San Diego *Herald.*

San Diego *Union.*

San Francisco *Bulletin.*

San Francisco *Call.*

San Francisco *Chronicle.*

Santa Barbara *Gazette.*

Southern Californian (Los Angeles).

Tidings (Los Angeles).

Weekly Bulletin (San Francisco).

IV. Periodical Works:

Clancy, Raymond J., C.S.C., "American Prelates at the Vatican Council," *Historical Records and Studies*, XXVIII, (New York, 1937), 7-135.

IV. PERIODICAL WORKS (Continued):

Corrigan, Owen B., "Rise of the Hierarchy in the United States," Catholic Historical Review, II, (October, 1916), 294-295.

Drennan, M. A., C.M., "The Early History of the Congregation of the Mission in Philadelphia," Records of the American Catholic Historical Society, XX, (December, 1908), 1-21.

Easterly, Frederick J., C.M., "The Vincentian Fathers," Thought Patterns, IX, (Saint John's University, 1961), 120-157.

Engel-Janosi, Friedrich, "The Successor of Pius IX," Catholic Historical Review, XXX, (April, 1944), 1-27.

Geiger, Maynard J., O.F.M., "The Apostolic College of Our Lady of Sorrows, Santa Barbara, 1853-1885," Provincial Annals (at irregular intervals).

Guilday, Peter, "Guide to the Bibliographical Sources of the American Hierarchy," Catholic Historical Review, V, (April, 1919), 122-128.

Ryan, Stephen V., "Early Lazarist Missions and Missionaries," Catholic Historical Magazine, I, (October, 1887), 366-387.

"Selections from the Correspondence of Mark Anthony Frenaye," Records of The American Catholic Historical Society, XIV, (1903- ?), 50-120.

Smith, Sara Trainer, "Sketch of Mary Brackett Willcox," Records of the American Catholic Historical Society, VII, (Winter, 1896), 395-453.

"The Beginnings of Catholicity in Cape Girardeau," Saint Louis Catholic Historical Review, III, (January-April, 1921), 51-75.

Tschan, Francis J., "The Catholic Church in the United States, 1852-1868," Records of the American Catholic Historical Society, LIX, (June, 1948), 77-117.

Vallete, Marc F., "Brief Sketch of Saint Charles Borromeo Seminary," United States Catholic Historical Magazine, I, 24.

Weber, Francis J., "An Historical Sketch of Saint Vibiana's Cathedral," Historical Society of Southern California Quarerly, XLIV (March, 1962), 53-56.

IV. PERIODICAL WORKS: *(continued)*:

Weber, Francis J., "Daughters of Charity in California," *The Daughter of Charity*, II, (December, 1963), 11-18.

Weber, Francis J., "Real Patronato de Indias," Historical Society of Southern California *Quarterly*, XLIII (June, 1961), 215-219.

Weber, Francis J., "Search for a Bishop," *Southern California Quarterly*, XLV (June, 1963), 8-14.

Weber, Francis J., "Thaddeus Amat—Fact versus Fiction," *Records of the American Catholic Historical Society*, LXXIV (September, 1963).

Weber, Francis J., "The Pious Fund of the Californias," *Hispanic American Historical Review*, XLIII (February, 1963), 78-94.

V. PRINTED SOURCES:

Aguilar, Mariano, *Historia de la Congregacion de las Hijas del SSMC Corazon de Maria*, Doria, Barcelona, 1909.

Amat, Thaddeus, C.M., *A Treatise on Matrimony*, Michael Flood, San Francisco, 1864.

Amat, Thaddeus, C.M., *Asociacion de Santa Vibiana . . .*, Imprenta de Pablo Riera, Barcelona, 1860.

Amat, Thaddeus, C.M., *Carta Pastoral* (Los Angeles, 1869, 1870 and 1873).

Amat, Thaddeus, C.M., *Exhortacion Pastoral* (Los Angeles, 1855, 1856).

Amat, Thaddeus, C.M., *Pastoral Letter* (Los Angeles, 1869, 1870, 1872 and 1873).

Amat, Thaddeus, C.M., *Reports of Saint Charles Seminary* (1848-1852), M. Fithian, Philadelphia, 1848 through 1852.

Amat, Thaddeus, C.M., *Tratado sobre el Matrimonio*, Barcelona, 1867.

Annales de le Congregation de la Mission, Paris, 1834.

Annuario Pontifico, (1860-1871), Tipografia Poliglotta, Rome, (issued as *La Gerarchin Cattolica* between 1872 and 1878).

Bancroft, Hubert Howe, *History of California*, 7 vols., The History Company, San Francisco, 1884-1889.

V. Printed Sources *(Continued)*:

Baudier, Roger, *The Catholic Church in Louisiana*, A. W. Hyatt, New Orleans, 1939.

Bayard, Ralph, C.M., *Lone Star Vanguard*, The Vincentian Press, Saint Louis, 1945.

Beiser, J. Ryan, *The Vatican Council and the American Secular Newspapers, 1869-1870*, The Catholic University of America Press, Washington, 1941.

Butler, Cuthbert, *The Vatican Council*, 2 vols., Longmans Green and Company, London, 1930.

Catalogue des Missions et du Personnell de la Congregation de la Mission, Paris, 1959.

Centennial Jubilee, Church of Saint Vincent de Paul, 1844-1944, Saint Louis, 1944.

Centennial Pageant Commemorating One Hundred Years of Progress—Perry County, 1827-1927, Missouri Printing Co., Cape Girardeau, 1927.

Chavez, Angelico, O.F.M., *Archives of the Archdiocese of Santa Fe*, Academy of American Franciscan History, Washington, 1957.

Code, Joseph B., *Dictionary of the American Hierarchy*, Longmans Green and Company, New York, 1940.

Conroy, Charles C., *The Centennial*, The Tidings Press, Los Angeles, 1940.

Curley, Michael J., *Venerable John Neumann, C.Ss.R.*, The Catholic University of America, Washington, 1952.

Enciclopedia Universale Ilustrada, Espasa-Calpe, Barcelona, 1952.

Engelhardt, Zephryin, O.F.M., *Missions and Missionaries*, 4 vols., James H. Barry Company, San Francisco, 1915.

Gabel, Richard J., *Public Funds for Church and Private Schools*, The Catholic University of America Press, Washington, 1937.

Geiger, Maynard J., O.F.M., *Calendar of Documents in the Santa Barbara Mission Archives*, Academy of American Franciscan History, Washington, 1947.

V. Printed Sources (Continued):

Gleeson, William, *History of the Catholic Church in California*, 2 vols., A. L. Bancroft Company, San Francisco, 1872.

Herrera, José, C.M., *Historia de la Congregacion de la Mision*, Editorial La Milagrosa, Madrid, 1949.

Hittell, Theodore H., *History of California*, N. J. Stone Company, San Francisco, 1885.

Hurley, Mark J., *Church-State Relationships in Education in California*, The Catholic University of America Press, Washington, 1948.

Kenneally, Finbar, O.F.M., *The Catholic Seminaries of California as Educational Institutions*, University of Toronto Press, Toronto, 1956.

Ludwig, Salvador, *Los Angeles in the Sunny Seventies*, Los Angeles, 1929.

Mansi, Jean Dominique, *Sacrorum Conciliorum nova et amplissima Collectio*, H. Welter, Leipzig, 1927.

Meehan, Thomas F., "Thaddeus Amat," in *The Catholic Encyclopedia*, I, 380-381, Robert Appleton, New York, 1907.

Newmark, Harris, *Sixty Years in Southern California*, Houghton-Mifflin Company, New York, 1930.

Nolan, Hugh J., *The Most Reverend Francis Peter Kenrick*, The Catholic University Press, Washington, 1948.

North, William E., *Catholic Education in Southern California*, The Catholic University of America Press, Washington, 1936.

Novena a Santa Vibiana, Virgen y Martir, Protectora de la Diocesis de Monterey, Vicente Torras, San Francisco, 1856.

O'Donnell, George, *Saint Charles Seminary*, Jeffries and Manz, Philadelphia, 1943 and 1953.

One Hundred Years of Service (The Daughters of Charity in California), n.p., 1956.

Paradela, Benito, C.M., *Notas Biograficas de los que han pertenacido a la Congregacion de la Mission en España*, Imprenta de Cleto Vallins, Madrid, 1935.

Reportoire Historique, Annales de la Congregation de la Mission, Paris, 1900.

V. Printed Sources (Continued):

Reuss, Francis X., Biographical Cyclopedia of the Catholic Hierarchy in the United States, M. H. Wilzius and Company, Milwaukee, 1898.

Rothensteiner, John, History of the Archdiocese of Saint Louis, Saint Louis, 1928.

Schulte, A. J., The Philadelphia Theological Seminary of Saint Charles Borromeo, (1832-1917), Catholic Standard and Times, Philadelphia, 1917.

Shea, John Gilmary, History of the Catholic Church in the United States, 4 vols., D. H. McBride Company, New York, 1892.

Shearer, Donald, O.F.M., Cap., Pontificia Americana, The Catholic University of America Press, Washington, 1932.

Sorrentini, Cayetano, Panegirico en honor de Santa Vibiana, Imprenta del Senor Adriano Le Clere, Paris, 1857.

Sweet, John, History of the Public School System of California, San Francisco, 1876.

Taylor, Alexander J., A Bibliography of Newspapers and Periodicals Published in California in 1855, edited by Douglas C. McMurtie, Evanston, 1943.

Three Centuries of Vincentian Missionary Labors (1617-1917), Miraculous Medal Press Association, 1917.

Vaughn, Dale G., El Obispo, Title Insurance and Trust Company, Los Angeles, 1929.

Weber, Francis J., "Bishop Amat at the Vatican Council," Educatio Cristiana, VII (Saint John's University, 1962).

INDEX

Adam, Joachim, 169
Aguilar, Cristobal, 124
Aguirre, Antonio, 83
Alaban, Domingo, 25
Alaya, Dina, 87
Alemany, Joseph Sadoc, 20, 28, 31, 34, 38, 40, 53, 57-71, 73-74, 130, 140, 142, 154, 168, 176, 179, 190, 196, 206ff.
All Hallows, College, 140, 187-188
Amat, Joaquin, 167
Amat, Jose, 2
Amat, Luigi, 2, 188
Amat, Pedro, 2
Amat, Thaddeus, Birth, 3; Religious life, 4; Profession in the Congregation of the Mission, 6; Ordained priest, 9; Departs for America, 10; Superior at Cape Girardeau, 13; Superior at Perryville, 13; Named Director of the Daughters of Charity in Madrid, 18; Transferred to Madrid, 19; Superior and Director of Daughters of Charity in Chile, 20; Consecrated bishop, 22; First Pastoral letter, 23; Arrives in California, 28, 34; Confers Pallium on Archbishop Alemany, 38-39; Installed at Monterey, 39; Ordains for first time in California, 43; Transfers seat to Los Angeles, 50; Franciscan controversy, 51-71; Engages in Pious Fund litigation, 73-83; Furthers diocesan expansion, 85-97; Brings Daughters of Charity to Los Angeles, 115-126; Installs Immaculate Heart Sisters in diocese, 126-129; Expands educational facilities, 129ff; Involved in Santa Ines Controversy, 140; Brings Congregation of the Mission to Los Angeles, 147-153; Acquires relics of Saint Vibiana, 157-162; Erects Cathedral, 162-169; Attends Vatican Council I, 171-185; Rumored as Archbishop of New Orleans, 189-190; Synodal activity, 190; Incorporates diocese, 203ff; Requests coadjutor, 206; Consecrates Francis Mora, 208; Dies, 213; Dis-interred, 214n; Eulogized, 214ff.
Anglo-Hispanic Conflict, xi
Arenas, Luis, 124
Armengol, Bonaventure, 11, 14
Ashley, D. R., 130
Assumption Seminary, 11-12
Asmuth, John, 149, 151

Barcelona, 1, 24, 50, 197
Barnabo, Alessandro, 48, 55, 61, 145, 197, 202
Bartlett, John, 95
Basso, John, 168
Beaudry, Prudent, 124
Bellarmine, Saint Robert, 215
Blanc, Anthony, 189
Bonaparte, Joseph, 3
Borica, Diego de, 137
Bouchard, James, 168
Brusi, Maria, 2
Bulla Cruciata, 48, 50
Burlando, Francis, 116, 122, 148ff

Cabrillo, Juan Rodriguez, 29
California, division of, xii note
Capdevila, Benito, 88
Caro, Francisco, 57ff
Casserly, Eugene, 75
Castellvell, Marquis de, 3
Catalonia, Province of, 1
Cavallier, Amiel, 165
Cervantes, Miguel de, 3

Childs, Ozro W., 153, 164
Claret, Saint Anthony, 127
Clark, Shulett, 89
Codina, Buenaventura, 18
College Ranch, 139
Congiato, Nicolas, 144
Conners, John, 131
Corporation Sole, 204ff
Corsina, Sr. Marie, 120
Croke, James, 77, 142, 145-146
Curran, Hugh, 92
Cushing, Caleb, 78

Daughters of Charity, 27, 40, 47, 49,
   115-126, 149, 164, 188, 202
Diario de Barcelona, 3
Dominican Sisters, 35
Donaldsonville, 11
Donohue, Thomas, 90
Downey, John, 118, 201
Doyle, John T., 74
Dupanloup, Felix, 173
Duran, Michael, 208

Emmanuel, King Victor II, 184
Escarra, Jose, 19
Escalante, Francisco, 141

Fauron, Victor, 88
Fernandez, Sr. Francisca, 120
Fernandez, Manuel, 212
Franchi, Alexander, 82
Francis II of Naples, 49
Franciscan Controversy, 51-71
Fransoni, Giacomo, 20, 22
Franzelin, Giovanni, 173
Fremont, John C., 123

Gallagher, Hugh, 117, 213
Garcia Diego, Francisco, 30, 35, 41, 42,
   62, 65, 74, 75, 199
Gillon, Sr. Ann, 120
Gold, discovery of, xii, 31
Guadalupe-Hidalgo, Treaty of, 76,78
Guerra, Don Jose de la, 33, 70 n

Hayes, Benjamin, 89, 200
Herrera, Dolores, 129
Holy Trinity Church, 13
Hotel des Lorges, 9, 26
Hudson, Thomas, 90
Hughes, John, 33, 48

Immaculate Heart Academy, 129

Immaculate Heart Church, 92
Immaculate Heart Sisters, 126-129, 206n
Indians, 63, 79, 93-97
Isabella, Queen, 7
Isabella II, Queen, 188

Jimeno, Antonio, 69
Jimeno, Jose, 65
Johnson, Andrew, 197
Jones, William, 212

Keane, William, 22
Kenrick, Francis Patrick, 14, 17, 26, 35
Kenrick, Peter Richard, 12n, 174
Kirby, Reverend Dr., 22
Kyser, E. F., 166

Leivicque, Vincent, 12
Lestrade, Anacletus, 43
Liguori, Saint Alphonsus, 61
Lincoln, Abraham, 86
Logsdon Sr. Mary Scholastica, 118, 121
Lootens, Louis, 190
Los Angeles Orphanage, 118ff
Loughlin, John, 145
Lugo, Don Vicente, 153

McCloskey, John, 174
McCloskey, William G., 189
McGill, James, 153, 165, 206
McQuaid, Bernard, 176

Maginnis, John, 115
Maguire, F. J., 123
Maller, Mariano, 15, 18
Mann, Horace, 129
Manning, Edward, 173
Masmitja, Joaquin, 127
Mathews, W. J., 166
Mesmer, Louis, 166
Micheltorena, Manuel, 30, 138ff
Mission San Luis Rey, 62, 200
Mission San Juan Capistrano, 166
Mission Santa Cruz, 87
Montefranco, Bernardino de, 61
Montgomery, Zacahariah, 125, 131
Mora, Francis, 26n, 91-92, 128, 129,
   166, 196, 205ff
Mumbardo, Sr. Angelita, 120

Nativity of the Blessed Virgin, Church
   of, 88
Neumann, Blessed John N., C. Ss. R.,
   17, 26

Nuestra Senora de la Merced, Iglesia de, 6
Neustra Senora del Pino, Iglesia de, 4
Newman, John Henry, 22
Newmark, Rose, 151
Nozo, John B., 11

O'Brien, Maurice, C. M., 91
O'Connell, Eugene, 140, 150, 190, 196, 207
Odin, John, 14, 190, 197
Oruno, Jesus, 65
Our Lady of Angels, Church of, 44-45, 189, 195, 201, 208, 213
Our Lady, Help of Christian, Church of, 91
Our Lady of Mount Carmel, Church of, Aptos, 92
Our Lady of Mount Carmel, Church of, 87
Our Lady of Refuge, Church of, 46
Our Lady of Sorrows, Church of, 40, 52, 69, 90, 160

Phelan, Gregory, 36
Phillips, Philip, 78
Piazza di Spagna, 22
Pious Fund, 30, 73-83
Pius IX, Pope, 24, 43, 55, 64, 157ff, 171ff, 190, 193, 198, 209
Plunkett, Blessed Oliver, 22
Puerto de San Miguel, Iglesia de, 166
Purcell, John B., 174, 206
Puggott, J., 149

Quelen, Hyacinthe Louise de, 10

Raho, Blasius, C. M., 13, 42, 44, 47, 49, 52, 88, 89, 132, 147, 188, 196
Ramirez, Don Pedro, 75
Rignano, Antonio di, 64
Romo, Joseph, O.F.M., 71
Rossi, Giovanni Battista de, 157
Rubi, Michael, 149, 154
Rubio, Cypriano, 128
Rubio, Gonzales, O.F.M., 30, 40, 42, 57-71, 140, 146, 199
Ryan, Stephen, 148ff

Sacred Heart Convent, 13
Saint Bernardine of Sienna, Church of, 90
Saint Boniface, Church of, 88
Saint Charles, Seminary of, 15

Saint Francis, Brothers of, 133
Saint Francis, Orphanage of, 92
Saint Ignatius, College, of, 32, 144
Saint Joseph, Academy of, 27
Saint Joseph, Chapel of, 88
Saint Joseph, Church of, 57
Saint Joseph, Church of (San Diego), 91
Saint Martin, Church of, 90
Saint Mary, Seminary of, 12-13
Saint Mary, Cathedral of, 38, 214
Saint Mary, Church of (Gilroy), 90, 128
Saint Mary, Church of (Visalia), 88
Saint Patrick, Church of, 92
Saint Peter, Church of, 90
Saint Vibiana, Cathedral of, 157-170, 213, 217
Saint Vincent, Church of (Saint Louis), 13
Saint Vincent, Church of (Los Angeles), 90
Saint Vincent, College of (Cape Girardeau), 12
Saint Vincent, College of (Los Angeles), 132, 147-153
Saint Vincent, Institution of, 123
Saint Vincent, Select School of, 153
Salhorgne, Dominic, 8
Salvador, Ludwig, 155
San Carlos Presidio Chapel, 39
San Emigdio, 88
San Jacinto, 89
San Juan Bautista Orphanage, 128
Sanchez, Francisco, O.F.M., 65
Santa Clara College, 32
Santa Eulalia Cathedral, 1
Santa Ines College, 57, 140
Santa Maria de Los Reyes (del Pino), 2
Sepulveda, Jose, 202
Serra, Junipero, 29, 96
Shorb, J. De Barth, 118
Sisnero, Sr. Clara, 120
Sisters of Mercy, 116
Sorrentini, Cajetan, 55, 56n, 61
Souhard, Antoine, Mansion of, 13
Spalding, Martin J., 172, 183, 192, 196
Swett, John, 131
Syllabus of Errors, 171

Taney, Roger B., 74
Thornton, Edward, 80
Timon, John, 13, 15, 18
Turchi, Lettorio, 22

Ubach, Anthony, 91, 96, 124
Ullathorne, William B., 185

Valencia, General, 75
Valle, Don Ignacio del, 120
Vatican Council I, 77, 127, 171-185, 195
Vaughn, Herbert, 34
Venisse, Edmond, 41
Verdaguer, Peter, 89
Vibiana, Saint, 26, 40, 43, 45, 91, 157-170

Vila, James, 123
Vincent de Paul, Saint, 5
Vinyes, Vincent, 206

Wadsworth, William, 79
Wilson, Benjamin D., 121
Wilson, Emily, 121
Wilson, Nathaniel, 78
Wiseman, Nicholas, 23

Yorba, Don Bernardo, 88